Homegrown With Love

MANSI AKRUWALA

To order additional copies of this book, contact:
Xlibris
844-714-8691
www.Xlibris.com
Orders@Xlibris.com

ISBN: Softcover   978-1-6641-6593-9
        Hardcover   978-1-6641-6594-6
        EBook   978-1-6641-6592-2

Print information available on the last page

Rev. date: 04/06/2021

Contents

Homegrown with Love

About the Author

Mansi was born and raised in New York and when she is not cooking up a culinary storm in her kitchen, she is working as a Medical Director. Mansi started her culinary adventures at the ripe age of 10, and some of her first creations were half-baked brownies in her Easy-Bake Oven and scrambled eggs made in the microwave. Through years of trial and error, tons of binging Food Network, and inspiration from countless recipes found through Instagram, Pinterest, and food blogs, Mansi has created many unique recipes of her own that she is thrilled to share with everyone. In her spare time, Mansi loves to travel and explore different cultures and most importantly, cuisines. Many of her creations are inspired by her travels, and her family gatherings.

Mansi has a very big family and one of her favorite pastimes is to cook for them. Her most notable culinary inspiration is her grandmother and Ina Garten. Mansi continues to pursue her passion for cooking and wants to convey how a home-cooked meal does not need to be complicated or intimidating.

One of her favorite quotes and life philosophies is something that Steve Jobs once said, *"Don't settle. As with all matters of the heart, you'll know when you find it."* Mansi became a doctor because helping people was something that she loved, and it was a career choice that she holds close to her heart. Similarly, cooking is a passion of hers and something that she truly feels was a calling. Mansi hopes to continue to share her love of food and enthusiasm for diverse flavors to her family and friends for many years to come.

Dedication

"Cooking is one of the great gifts you can give to those you love."
-Ina Garten

This cookbook is for my family and friends, for whom I will always enjoy cooking for, with so much love, enthusiasm, and passion. These recipes warm my heart and soul and are meant to honor my late grandmother's legacy. And for every other beginner, novice, or seasoned chef, this cookbook is for you to start your own culinary and family traditions. For every great meal is homegrown, with love.

To my loving, supportive, and always entertaining family, whom never cease to make me laugh and smile and who have supported me in every one of my endeavors-thank you, for everything, always.

To my big love and partner in life, Manish-thank you for always being my culinary adventure buddy, and for occasionally frying my paneer for me when I am too scared. Would not have it any other way.

Love, Mansi

Bhabhi
1983

Bhabhi and I
2011

My Dad and I
1990

My Parents, Sister, and I
1994

My Parents and I in Spain
2019

My Family
2021

Manish and I
2021

The OG Mom Cooks
1990

Introduction

When I was young, I used to carefully watch my grandmother, whom we lovingly called "Bhabhi", cook in the kitchen. She was so calculated, meticulous, almost scientific, but there was also something so free and charismatic about her as she whisked back and forth in the kitchen, with her lavender saree flowing about. Her favorite color was lavender, and it embodied the serenity she carried with her always. I still remember the disarray her masala dabba (container) was constantly in because she would use it so often. The masala dabba is so ubiquitous in Indian homes and brings with it years of family tradition and symbolism. Every spice is used for a specific need, often for the benefit of one's health. My grandmother never measured anything but somehow, she always got the proportions just right. She taught me that people often eat with their eyes first, so colors and presentation were as equally as important as the flavors.

If I close my eyes, I can still smell the aromas of the spices and masalas she used and taste the bold, rich flavors she would develop. And most importantly, I can still feel the way she made me feel through her cooking. She conveyed a tangible connection and feeling to her food. But it was not just the love I felt, it was her passion, and her ability to tell a story through her food. She was the first person to teach me the art of cooking. Maya Angelou said it so perfectly, "People will forget what you said, people will forget what you did, but people will never forget how you made them feel." Even as I write this, and think about her I am filled with so many emotions and warm memories. The feeling is simply indescribable, but I know that she is here with me. Her presence and support is always felt. I also know that she is so proud of me and all of her grandchildren, who have all gone on to achieve so many wonderful things in life.

It was through her food that I first learned the importance of tradition and family. She had a very difficult life in a small village in India, Viramgam. She experienced the hardest of times and remained so resilient in the face of adversity and struggle. She was left a young widow with 6 small, and active children to feed, and yet somehow even with so little, she managed to instill in me that food was not simply for sustenance. As people, we have evolved to associate food with a symbolic meaning and profound significance. In fact, when I was in my undergraduate I took a course at NYU in the Anthropology department and it was called "Culture Through Food". It was fascinating to learn about so many different cultures and how food played such a significant role in them. Food was and still is at the center of my family. We gather and have meals together as a family and celebrate milestones, holidays, and occasions, all with the central focus on food and the love for one another.

My passion for cooking started at a young age and began with KRAFT mac and cheese from the box and scrambled eggs in the microwave. I also cannot forget about my trusty but finicky Easy-Bake Oven I had as a small child. Many a raw brownies were eaten from that oven. I also used to love watching my mom and my aunts cook for 50 people in the kitchen, they always worked as a team and made it seem effortless. As I got older, I started to get more creative and became obsessed with the Food Network. I grew up watching Emeril Lagasse and was intrigued by his recipes, but even more so his zest for cooking and his enthusiasm that grew with every "BAM!".

When I was in high school, I fell in love with Ina Garten and the home-cooked meals she would prepare with so much love and joy for her sweet husband Jeffrey. I thought, now there is a couple that truly embodies love. I was in awe of her food, her sweet smile and calm demeanor, and her tablescapes were always ones to envy. She is the GOAT of entertainers. I was convinced that one day I would be invited to one of her beautiful garden parties that she would often host for her dear friends. I am still holding on to that dream. She once said, "I like to greet my friends with a drink in my hand, a warm smile on my face, and great music in the background because that's what gets a dinner party off to a fun start." And I remember thinking, what a wonderful approach she had. She even claimed to be a "scientist at heart", and I felt so connected to her and I completely understood what she meant. Ina taught me that generally speaking, "store bought is fine", and to always to use "good vanilla". She once said, "food is not about impressing people, it is about making them feel comfortable", and this resonated so deeply with me. Food should feel like home and bring a familial comfort.

Later, my obsession with Chopped developed and I could binge these episodes for hours. The ingenuity of these chefs, the brow sweat inducing time constraints, and the bizarre ingredients they would find in their baskets would give me goose bumps, but they kept me so intrigued. I was beyond inspired by Chopped. Somehow, these chefs could transform bacon-flavored ice cream, licorice, and kale into a culinary experience. They were innovative, creative, and risk takers, and all of these were qualities I aspired to develop for my own cooking. My favorite judges were also chefs whom have always inspired me, such as Alex Guarnaschelli, Scott Conant, and Geoffrey Zakarian.

Over the years, thanks to social media, I have become quite creative and innovative in the meals that I prepare. I draw on so many different cultures, chefs, food blogs, cooking shows, cookbooks, and recipes for inspiration. There is not a single cuisine that I do not like, nor one that I have not experimented with in my own kitchen. I loved the movie "Julie and Julia", I felt transported to Julia Child's kitchen and her quirky demeanor was so endearing. Her love for her husband reminded me of Ina and Jeffrey. Julia Child was wonderful. Cooking is more than a passion for me and more than a mere hobby. It is a cathartic experience. Just to be able to walk into my kitchen and prepare something completely from scratch and then watch my loved ones enjoy the food over good laughs and stories is incredible. My favorite holiday is Thanksgiving and everyone who knows me knows that it is my Super Bowl. It is the event of the year for me because it combines everything I love and am passionate about-family, food, and football. It has been a tradition for me to make a menu of 15 to 20 dishes and I cook it all by myself on Thanksgiving Day. Nothing gives me more joy than seeing my family enjoy the food that I have prepared for them. Thanksgiving is my way of showing the gratitude and love that I have for my family and acknowledging their support and ongoing presence in my life.

When I became a physician, I found myself in the kitchen, forgoing the precision that is often so prevalent and necessary in medicine. The kitchen became a place where rules and measurements were mere guidelines, or loose constraints. But I also discovered many parallels between medicine and cooking that existed and emerged the more I cooked. Just as many grey areas exist in medicine, and lines are often blurred or even smudged, I found that in the kitchen, the same rules of chaos reigned free. Eyeballing became a much-welcomed philosophy, and frankly a reprieve from a lifestyle and career of cognizant precision and accuracy. Just like in medicine, nothing is certain, and perfection is a subjective term. The bottom line was often smudged and it was not missed one bit.

My goal in wanting to develop my own cookbook is not for fame or notoriety, or even to make a quick buck. This is my passion project-something that I could carefully curate and develop with so much love and patience. It has been a truly humbling, gratifying, and educational process. I loved the creativity that this process allowed for me to explore. All of these photographs were personally styled by me, and so aesthetically pleasing. I was able to combine my passion for cooking and love for art. Special thanks to reruns of Curb Your Enthusiasm and my Spotify for keeping me company while I cooked into the late hours, and many times early mornings. Larry David is my spirit animal and he kept me laughing and entertained through this whole process, and the result I think is "pretty, pretty, pretty good".

This cookbook was developed with the everyday person in mind. Whether it is a working mother of two, or a college student on a budget, these recipes are meant to be recreated and enjoyed by all. I want people to know that cooking does not need to be intimidating, and that it can be really fun. Cooking should be accessible to all, regardless of their experience level or budget. You do not need to have studied at the Cordon Bleu or even have successfully mastered Julia Child's beef bourguignon or her French silk pie. You do not even need to poach an egg! And you definitely do not need to truffle hunt with dogs or summon milk from the dairy farms of Amsterdam to obtain quality ingredients to cook with. This cookbook is an amalgam of the places I have traveled to around the world and the different cuisines and cultures that I have explored. In here, you will find vegetarian recipes for Indian, Japanese, Chinese, Mexican, Italian, Greek, Middle Eastern, and American cuisines. These recipes are about bold, rich flavors, culinary adventures around the world, comfort food, family, and most importantly, they are all homemade with love.

Ultimately, this cookbook is a way of honoring my grandmother who meant so much to me and whose loss I continue to feel and whose memories I hold so dear even as the years pass. She taught me that food is meant to celebrate life with. This cookbook is to honor my grandmother's legacy in all of the ways that she has influenced and inspired me. And most importantly, it is my way to show all of you the values that she had instilled in me. I hope that by sharing these recipes, I can share my love and passion for cooking but also my heritage, culture, and family values.

Hopefully, you will see that my recipes are indeed, "Homegrown With Love".

Buon appetito.

With love,
Mansi

Bhabhi
1943

Masala Daaba

Bhabhi
1983

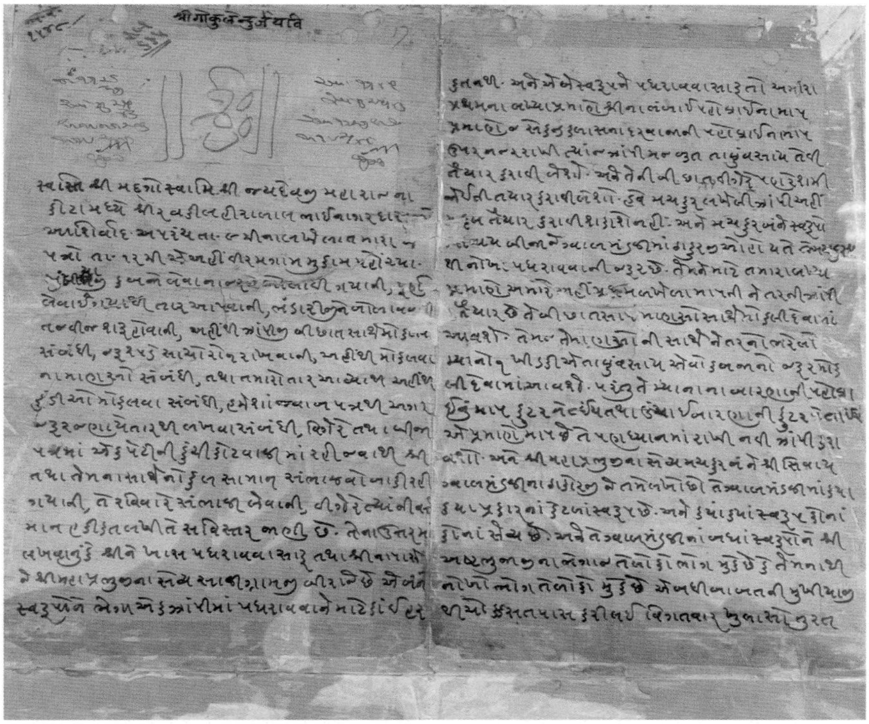
श्रीगोकुलेन्दुर्जयति

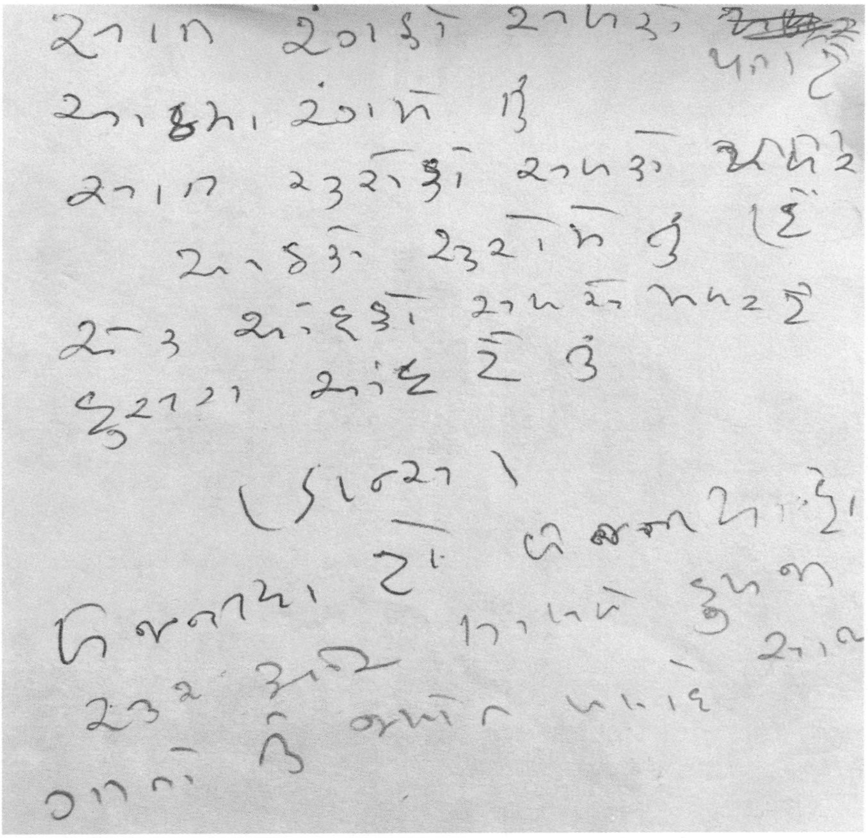

Behind the Scenes

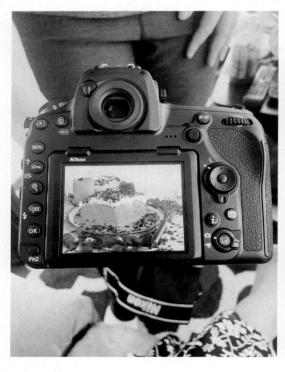

Acknowledgements

Sarah-Ann Hamlin is the photographer behind these stunning shots. She lives in New Hampshire with her husband and 5 children. Sarah started out mostly shooting portrait photography and while that is still her main focus, she was excited to work together to begin her foray into food photography. I am incredibly grateful for her talent and the time that she dedicated to this cookbook. Thank you, Sarah.

To all of my friends, family, and kind strangers who I have met along this incredible journey-Thank you all, from the bottom of my heart. Thank you for your support and encouragement, as none of this would be possible without it.

Love,
Mansi

Cauliflower Shawarma

This is the recipe for those of you who are in constant pursuit of flavor and fusion of those flavors, like me. I call this meal the "perfect date night meal" because it is so easy to make and presents beautifully with the appropriately paired sides. For this dish, I drew on Middle Eastern and Indian flavor profiles to create a unique and innovative dish that really will make your mouth water. I hope to see this recipe recreated and captured, because it is truly a personal favorite of mine. For a good music recommendation for your date night, anything by Nancy Ajram is a must especially if it is ya tabtab wa dallaa.

Prep time 10 minutes
Cook time 35 minutes
Servings 4
Total Time 50 minutes

Mansi Akruwala

INGREDIENTS

Cauliflower shawarma

- 1 large head cauliflower, cut into florets
- 1/4 cup extra-virgin olive oil
- 4 cloves garlic, minced or grated
- 2 teaspoons cayenne pepper
- 2 tablespoons ground cumin
- 1 teaspoon fennel powder
- 2 tablespoons garam masala powder
- 2 teaspoons black pepper
- 2 tablespoons zaatar seasoning
- 3-4 tablespoons chickpea flour or besan
- 1 tablespoon sesame seeds
- 2 teaspoons smoked paprika
- 2 tablespoons tandoori masala or chicken tikka masala
- Himalayan pink salt to taste
- 2-3 tablespoons labneh or Greek yogurt
- Cilantro for garnish
- Pita or naan for serving
- Cilantro and jalapeño hummus
- Water to thin out marinade

Green tahini sauce

- ¼ cup tahini sesame paste
- 2-3 cloves of garlic
- ¼ cup extra-virgin olive oil
- ½ cup Greek yogurt
- 1 cup fresh cilantro
- 2 tablespoons fresh squeezed lemon juice
- 2 teaspoons cumin powder
- Salt to taste

Cucumber and Tomato Salad

- ½ diced seedless English cucumber
- 1 ripe vine tomato, chopped
- 2 tablespoons extra-virgin olive oil
- 2 teaspoons tzatziki seasoning
- Feta cheese, crumbled
- Salt and black pepper to taste

INSTRUCTIONS

1. Preheat oven or air fryer to 425 degrees F.

2. On a baking sheet, combine the cauliflower, 1/4 cup olive oil, minced or grated garlic, cumin, cayenne pepper, garam masala, tandoor or chicken tikka masala, black pepper, fennel powder and salt to taste. Then add the labneh or Greek yogurt and toss well to evenly coat. Next, add the chickpea flour or besan. You can marinate the cauliflower for 30 minutes if you would like, but this step is not essential and can be omitted. Alternatively, this cauliflower can be marinaded and stored in the refrigerator and baked when ready. Add the sesame seeds and gently toss. Transfer to the oven and roast or air fry for 35 minutes, or until tender and lightly charred. Roasting or air frying times may vary depending on your individual oven, so adjust accordingly. Your kitchen will become very aromatic at this point. Enjoy the aromas.

3. In the meantime, you may prepare the cilantro and jalapeño hummus and the green tahini to pair with the cauliflower shawarma. For the green tahini sauce, in a food processor or blender, add the tahini sesame paste, olive oil, lemon juice, Greek yogurt, cilantro, and salt to taste. For the hummus, follow the recipe in the book. For the Cucumber and Tomato salad, combine the cucumbers, tomato, feta, olive oil, tzatziki seasoning, and salt and black pepper to taste. You may also make or heat up fresh pita bread to serve with. Tastes great on its own too.

4. To serve, spread the hummus first on the warm pita or naan, then add the roasted cauliflower shawarma and finish with a generous drizzle of green tahini, more sesame seeds, and cayenne pepper or paprika on top. Then add the fresh cilantro garnish. Serve with the Cucumber and Tomato Salad. Fresh chopped mint or mint chutney would also work well with this dish.

5. Enjoy your date night!

Cilantro and Jalapeño Hummus

This Cilantro and Jalapeño Hummus is incredibly flavorful, fragrant, and creamy. It pairs perfectly with the Cauliflower Shawarma recipe but can also be served with pita and veggies for a quick but delicious appetizer. This recipe is great because it is easy to scale and serve a party of 2 or 20. This recipe also allows for modifications to produce the flavor profile of choice. Some people, myself included, like to go heavy on the tahini paste and garlic. This hummus also has a beautiful light green hue and is guaranteed to be a party pleaser.

- ✎ Prep time 5 minutes
- ⏱ Cook time 5 minutes
- 🍴 Servings 2-3
- 🕐 Total time 10 minutes

INGREDIENTS

CILANTRO AND JALAPEÑO HUMMUS

- 1 15.5 oz can of chickpeas
- ¼ cup tahini sesame paste
- ½ cup Greek yogurt
- 3 cloves of garlic
- 2 tablespoons fresh squeezed lemon juice
- ¼ cup extra-virgin olive oil, adjust amount for creamy consistency
- 1 jalapeño, de-seeded, adjust according to desired spice level
- 1 cup of fresh cilantro
- 2 teaspoons cumin powder
- Paprika, for garnish

INSTRUCTIONS

1. In a food processor, blend together the rinsed chickpeas, tahini paste, cumin powder, Greek yogurt, garlic, fresh squeezed lemon juice, extra-virgin olive oil, jalapeño, and cilantro. Add salt to taste.

2. Pour hummus into a decorative bowl and top with cilantro and drizzle olive oil and paprika on top.

3. Serve and enjoy with some warm pita or Cauliflower Shawarma.

Paneer Tikka Tacos

These paneer tikka tacos are everything that anyone would crave from a fusion dish. Mexican tacos were my inspiration but I wanted to elevate them with an Indian flair and I felt like paneer was the perfect vehicle. This dish brings forward the culinary flavors of both India and Mexico and the colors and flavors remind me of such cultures as well. These tacos are a must on "Taco Tuesday" and are also great for entertaining with. Whip up some fresh guac and some hibiscus margaritas and you have got yourself a fiesta. I love the idea of these tacos for a girls night in, featuring your favorite 90s romcom (She's All That or 10 Things I Hate About You are musts), and some homemade avocado and cucumber facial masks. Quirky friends, salacious gossip, and 90s eye candy not included with these tacos, but always encouraged.

- Prep time 15 minutes
- Cook time 30 minutes
- Servings 5
- Total time 1 hour and 25 minutes

INGREDIENTS

PANEER TIKKA TACOS

- 1 14 oz. low-fat paneer slab
- 2 tablespoons tandoori masala
- 1 tablespoon garam masala
- 3 tablespoons fenugreek leaves or kasoori methi
- 2 tablespoons chaat masala
- 2 tablespoons cumin powder
- 2 tablespoons red chili powder or mirchi
- 1 tablespoon turmeric powder
- 1 tablespoon fennel powder
- Salt and black pepper to taste
- 1 cup of Greek or desi yogurt
- ¼ cup cilantro, finely chopped
- 3-4 tablespoons of chickpea flour or besan
- ¼ cup extra-virgin olive oil
- Small flour tortillas
- Chopped iceberg lettuce
- Cilantro for garnish

TANDOORI ONIONS

- 1 red onion
- 1 tablesoon ghee or cooking oil of choice
- 1 tablespoon cumin powder
- 2 tablespoons tandoori masala
- 2 tablespoons chaat masala
- Salt to taste

CILANTRO AND JALAPEÑO CREMA

- 1 cup fresh cilantro
- ½ cup of Greek yogurt
- 2 tablespoons cumin powder
- 1 tablespoon red chili powder or mirchi
- 2 tablespoons taco seasoning
- 2-3 cloves of garlic
- ½ jalapeño, de-seeded (optional)
- 1 tablespoon fresh squeezed lemon juice

INSTRUCTIONS

1. Pre-heat oven or air fryer to 425 degrees F.

2. Cube the paneer slab into 1-2 inch cubes and thinly slice the red onion.

3. In a mixing bowl, combine all of the spices as follows, cumin powder, turmeric powder, red chili powder or mirchi, tandoori masala, fennel powder, chaat masala, kasoori methi, garam masala, and salt and pepper to taste. Then add the extra-virgin olive oil, Greek or desi yogurt and besan or chickpea flour. Add in fresh chopped cilantro. Finally, toss in the paneer cubes. Allow mixture to marinade for 30 min.

4. Place the marinaded paneer cubes onto a baking sheet and bake or air-fry for 30 minutes, until aromatic, and slightly charred and crispy. Baking times will vary depending on individual ovens, so adjust accordingly.

5. In a pan, on medium heat, sauté the garlic in olive oil until fragrant, add in the sliced red onions. Next, add in the cumin powder, chaat masala, tandoori masala, and garam masala. Add salt to taste.

6. For the Cilantro and Jalapeño Crema, blend together Greek yogurt, cilantro, cumin powder, garlic, red chili powder or mirchi, taco seasoning, the jalapeño and salt to taste.

7. Prepare the tacos. Warm the flour tortillas on a grill, getting nice char marks. Next add the baked paneer tikka pieces. Next, add the sautéed tandoori onions, and chopped iceberg lettuce. Finally, generously drizzle the Cilantro and Jalapeño Crema.

8. Serve the Paneer Tikka Tacos and a festive platter and complete the meal with your favorite house-made guacamole and some hibiscus margaritas.

9. Enjoy the tacos with your girlfriends while you proceed to drool at Freddie Prinze Jr. for the next 1 hour and 30 minutes.

Roasted Brussels Sprout Tacos

These Roasted Brussels Sprout Tacos are also a great dish to entertain guests with and another option for "Taco Tuesday". Brussels sprouts are part of the cruciferous vegetable family and get their name from the cross that is made from their 4 petals. These vegetables contain glucosinolates, which are being studied for their benefits in cancer treatments. I absolutely love brussels sprouts especially in the Fall, and during Thanksgiving. They are great when roasted or fried and take on so much incredible flavor. They can be crispy or raw, and often give off a nutty flavor. These tacos are paired with the most delicious Caramelized Shallot and Cherry Tomato Salsa and topped with Spanish-sheep's milk manchego cheese which is creamy and tangy. These tacos are worth the little effort and will leave you and your dinner guests wanting more. Pair with some good rioja or some passion fruit margaritas, and don't feel bad if you take a siesta after these tasty tacos.

Prep time 10 minutes
Cook time 30 minutes
Servings 4
Total time 45 minutes

INGREDIENTS

Roasted Brussel Sprouts Tacos

- 1 10 oz. bag of shaved brussels sprouts
- 2 tablespoons extra-virgin olive oil
- 2-3 cloves of garlic, crushed or grated
- 2 tablespoons cumin powder
- 2 tablespoons taco seasoning
- Salt and black pepper to taste
- Small flour tortillas
- 4 oz. of Manchego cheese

Caramelized Shallot and Cherry Tomato Salsa

- 4 shallots, sliced
- 1 pint grape tomatoes, halved
- 2 tablespoons extra-virgin olive oil
- 2 tablespoons cumin powder
- 2 tablespoons taco seasoning
- 3 cloves of garlic
- 1 cup cilantro, chopped
- ½ jalapeño, de-seeded
- ½ cup salsa verde, store bought or homemade

Cilantro and Jalapeño Crema

- 1 cup fresh cilantro
- ½ cup of Greek yogurt
- 2 tablespoons cumin powder
- 2-3 cloves of garlic
- ½ jalapeño, de-seeded (optional)
- 1 tablespoon fresh squeezed lemon juice

INSTRUCTIONS

1. Pre-heat oven or air fryer to 375 degrees F.

2. On a baking sheet, lay out the shaved brussels sprouts with the crushed or grated garlic, and coat with extra-virgin olive oil. Then add cumin powder, taco seasoning and salt and black pepper to taste. Bake in the oven for 30 minutes, until aromatic and lightly charred and crispy.

3. In the meantime, grill the flour tortillas, developing some good char marks. Also, shred the manchego cheese and reserve on the side.

4. For the salsa, slice the shallots, cut the grape tomatoes in half, and chop the jalapeño. Place it all on a baking sheet with some extra-virgin olive oil, cumin powder, taco seasoning, and salt and black pepper to taste. Bake the salsa for 30 minutes as well. Once cooled a bit, transfer the salsa to a bowl and add in the fresh chopped cilantro.

5. For the Cilantro and Jalapeño Crema, blend together Greek yogurt, cumin powder, taco seasoning, garlic, jalapeño cilantro, and lemon juice with salt to taste.

6. Take the warm, slightly charred flour tortillas and begin to build your tacos. Add the roasted brussels sprouts first. Then add the Caramelized Shallot and Cherry Tomato Salsa. Drizzle on the Cilantro and Jalapeño Crema, and top with shredded manchego cheese.

7. Enjoy the tacos with a nice glass of wine and feel free to give in to the food coma that is surely to come.

Mushroom Tacos Al Pastor

Tacos al pastor are traditional tacos served in Mexico with a spit-grilled pork. Many people do not know that the flavor profile of this dish was influenced by the Lebanese immigrants to Mexico who would make lamb shawarma. The pork is first marinated in dried guajillo chilies, garlic, cumin, clove, bay leaf, and pineapple and then roasted over a charcoal pit. I have always been incredibly drawn to these flavors and who doesn't love a great taco? Since I am vegetarian, I decided to recreate these tacos in the al pastor flavor profile. The result was as delectable as it sounds. Perfect meal for Meatless Mondays.

Prep time 10 minutes
Cook time 30 minutes
Servings 4
Total time 45 minutes

INGREDIENTS

MUSHROOM TACOS AL PASTOR

- 1 8 oz. of baby bella mushrooms
- 2 tablespoons extra-virgin olive oil
- 3 cloves of garlic, crushed or grated
- 2 tablespoons cumin powder
- 2 tablespoons taco seasoning
- ½ jalapeño, de-seeded
- 1 7 oz. can of chipotle peppers in adobo sauce
- ½ cup of pineapple chunks with juice
- ½ cup cilantro
- 2 shallots
- Salt and black pepper to taste
- Small flour tortillas
- 4 oz. of crumbled cotija cheese
- Avocado slices with lime, for garnish

CILANTRO AND JALAPEÑO CREMA

- 1 cup fresh cilantro
- ½ cup of Greek yogurt
- 2 tablespoons cumin powder
- 2 tablespoons taco seasoning
- 2-3 cloves of garlic
- ½ jalapeño, de-seeded (optional)
- 1 tablespoon fresh squeezed lime juice

INSTRUCTIONS

1. Pre-heat oven or air fryer to 375 degrees F.

2. Slice the baby bella mushrooms and the shallots, thinly. In a blender, add the chipotle peppers in adobo sauce, pineapple chunks and their juice, garlic cloves, cumin powder, taco seasoning, and jalapeño. Blend until smooth, add more or less pineapple juice for creamy sauce consistency.

3. On medium heat, sauté the garlic and shallots until fragrant, add in the sliced baby bella mushrooms. Cook until tender about 10-12 minutes. Then add in the al pastor sauce that you previously made and let simmer for 15 minutes.

4. In the meantime, grill the flour tortillas, developing some good char marks.

5. For the Cilantro and Jalapeño Crema, blend together Greek yogurt, cumin powder, garlic, jalapeño cilantro, and lemon juice with salt to taste.

6. Take the warm, slightly charred flour tortillas and begin to build your tacos. Add the mushrooms al pastor first. Drizzle on the Cilantro and Jalapeño Crema, and top with crumbled cotija cheese and sliced avocados with a squeeze of lime and salt.

7. Enjoy the tacos with some spicy guava margaritas with a red chili sugar rim.

Roasted Butternut Squash Tacos with Curried Goat Cheese

There is nothing I love more about the Fall than the colorful leaves, cool, crisp air, the amazing fashion filled with chic sweaters, cute boots, and scarves, and of course the food. I also cannot forget my favorite holiday, which also happens to be in my favorite season, Fall-Thanksgiving. The Fall has many wonderful hearty and nutritious vegetables to offer, and my favorite of them all would have to be butternut squash. Roasted butternut squash is so flavorful and nutty and has a hint of sweetness. I decided to create a taco that honors my love of both butternut squash and goat cheese, my most favorite creamy and tangy cheese. These tacos are a bit of Fall with a delicious Indian twist.

- 🖊 Prep time 10 minutes
- 🍲 Cook time 45 minutes
- 🍴 Servings 4
- 🕐 Total time 1hour

Mansi Akruwala

INGREDIENTS

ROASTED BUTTERNUT SQUASH TACOS

- 1 15 oz. pre-cut butternut squash cubes
- 2 tablespoons extra-virgin olive oil
- 3 cloves of garlic, crushed or grated
- 2 tablespoons cumin powder
- 2 tablespoons taco seasoning
- 2 tablespoons tandoori masala
- 2 tablespoons garam masala

TANDOORI ONIONS

- 1 red onion
- 1 tablesoon ghee or cooking oil of choice
- 1 tablespoon cumin powder
- 2 tablespoons tandoori masala
- 2 tablespoons chaat masala
- Salt to taste

CURRIED GOAT CHEESE

- 1 4 oz goat cheese log
- 2 tablespoons cumin powder
- 2 tablespoons turmeric powder
- 2 tablespoons red chili powder or mirchi
- 2 tablespoons chaat masala
- 2 tablespoons garam masala
- 2 cloves of garlic, crushed or grated
- 1/2 cup fresh cilantro
- Salt and Pepper to taste

INSTRUCTIONS

1. Pre-heat oven or air fryer to 375 degrees F.

2. Take the pre-cut butternut squash cubes and mix with olive oil, crushed garlic, cumin powder, taco seasoning, garam masala, tandoori masala, and chaat masala. Roast in the oven for 45 minutes, until tender and charred.

3. In a pan, on medium heat, sauté the garlic in olive oil until fragrant, then add the cumin powder, turmeric, red chili powder, garam masala, and chaat masala. Mix together and then turn off heat. Add in the fresh chopped cilantro.

4. In another pan, on medium heat, sauté the garlic in olive oil until fragrant, add in the sliced red onions. Next, add in the cumin powder, chaat masala, tandoori masala, and garam masala. Add salt to taste.

5. In the meantime, grill the flour tortillas, developing some good char marks.

6. Take the warm charred flour tortilla and prepare your tacos. First, spread the Curried Goat Cheese on it. Then add the roasted butternut squash. Next, add the tandoori onions on top. And finally, top with iceberg lettuce and add more of the curried goat cheese and cilantro on top.

7. Enjoy the tacos with some tamarind margaritas and your favorite 90s Bollywood movie (Dil Toh Pagal Hai is an all time favorite of mine).

Tandoori Paneer Naan Pizza

Friday night is usually pizza night at my house, and sometimes I like to mix it up. This Tandoori Paneer Naan is exactly the kind of Friday night pizza for when you want to shake it up and bring some flavor. The tandoori paneer can be marinaded in advance and stored in the refrigerator for at least 3-4 days. This a great meal to plan ahead and makes for a fun and easy Friday night dinner. Also, great to entertain friends with.

- Prep time 10 minutes
- Cook time 30 minutes
- Servings 4 servings
- Total time 45 minutes

INGREDIENTS

TANDOORI PANEER NAAN PIZZA

- 1 cup Hot and Sweet Maggie sauce
- 1 cup tomato sauce
- 1 14 oz. low-fat paneer slab
- 2 tablespoons tandoori masala
- 2 tablespoons garam masala
- 3 tablespoons fenugreek leaves or kasoori methi
- 2 tablespoons chaat masala
- 2 tablespoons cumin powder
- 2 tablespoons red chili powder or mirchi
- 2 tablespoons of fennel powder
- Salt and black pepper to taste
- ½ cup of Greek yogurt
- 3-4 tablespoons of chickpea flour or besan
- ¼ cup extra-virgin olive oil
- 1 red onion
- 1 tablespoon ghee or cooking oil of choice
- 1 tablespoon cumin powder
- 2 tablespoons tandoori masala
- 2 tablespoons chaat masala
- Salt to taste
- 4 frozen naans
- Mozzarella cheese, shredded
- Amul cheese, shredded
- Cilantro, to garnish
- Chaat masala, to garnish

INSTRUCTIONS

1. Pre-heat the oven to 375 degrees F.

2. Cube the paneer slab into 1-2 inch cubes and thinly slice the red onion.

3. In a mixing bowl, combine all of the spices as follows, cumin powder, red chili powder or mirchi, tandoori masala, fennel powder, chaat masala, kasoori methi, garam masala, and salt and pepper to taste. Then add the extra-virgin olive oil, Greek yogurt and besan or chickpea flour. Finally, toss in the paneer cubes. Allow mixture to marinade for 30 min.

4. Place the marinaded paneer cubes onto a baking sheet and bake for 30 minutes, until aromatic, and slightly charred and crispy. Baking times will vary depending on individual ovens, so adjust accordingly.

5. In a pan, on medium heat, sauté the garlic in olive oil until fragrant, add in the sliced red onions. Next, add in the cumin powder, chaat masala, tandoori masala, and garam masala. Add salt to taste.

6. For the sauce, in a pan, on medium heat. Sauté the garlic in olive oil, until fragrant. Then add the Hot and Sweet Maggie Sauce and the tomato sauce. Stir to combine and let cook for 10-15 minutes. This can be done while the paneer is baking in the oven.

7. Assemble the pizza. Spread the sauce first, then the tandoori paneer and the tandoori onions. Top with mozzarella and Amul cheeses. Then bake in oven for about 15-20 minutes until cheese has melted and the pizza is crispy. Top with cilantro and chaat masala.

8. Enjoy the pizza with a nice cold can of Thums up (a personal favorite, somehow Indian soda is just better), and while watching your favorite Friday night movie.

Mexican Lasagna

Turn up the reggaeton, some Becky G or J Balvin will do, and put your apron on, and get cooking!

I absolutely love a traditional Italian lasagna with my vegetarian twist. I make the sauce from San Marzano tomatoes and lots of fresh garlic and basil. For the filling I mix ricotta cheese with spinach, garlic, fresh basil, and zucchini, and then I blend this into a creamy green mixture. My trick for delicious lasagna is a mix of processed shredded mozzarella and fresh mozzarella. My lasagna is hands down of my favorite things to make and it is always enjoyed at big family gatherings because it is so easy to make ahead of time and bake when needed. This Mexican Lasagna is a spin on the classic and is bursting with flavor. It is easy to make, but just requires some extra steps. Like most of my dishes, this lasagna is meant to be made in bulk and enjoyed during big family gatherings. Passion fruit margaritas are a must. Keep that reggaeton on blast and enjoy making this dish while dancing through your kitchen with a drink in your hand.

- 🔪 Prep time 10 minutes
- ⏱ Cook time 45 minutes
- 🍴 Servings 6-8 servings
- 🕐 Total time 1 hour 15 minutes

Mansi Akruwala

INGREDIENTS

- 2 15 oz. cans of black beans
- 1 box of 9 oz. oven-ready lasagne noodles
- 4 cloves garlic, minced or crushed
- 1 yellow onion, diced
- 2 tablespoons olive oil
- 3 tablespoons tomato paste
- 2-3 tablespoons of taco seasoning
- 2 tablespoons cumin powder
- Salt and black pepper to taste
- ¼ cup fresh cilantro
- 1 cup of homemade or store bought salsa
- 1 cup of water
- 1 7 oz. can of chipotle peppers in adobo sauce
- 1 8 oz. package of light cream cheese
- 1 bottle of salsa verde
- ½ pound extra sharp cheddar cheese
- 1 red onion, thinly sliced
- 1 jalapeño, de-seeded and sliced
- 1 avocado, sliced
- Fresh lemon
- Cilantro, to garnish
- Iceburg lettuce, thinly shredded

INSTRUCTIONS

1. Pre-heat the oven to 375 degrees F.

2. Sauté garlic in olive oil, until fragrant. Add in the onions, cilantro, and then the tomato paste. Allow the mixture to cook for 5 minutes. Then add in the rinsed black beans, cumin, taco seasoning, and black beans. Finally, add 1 cup of water. Add more depending on how creamy you want the black beans. Allow the beans to cook for 15 to 20 minutes then blend with an immersion or hand blender until smooth and creamy.

3. For the chipotle sauce, simply mix the chipotle peppers in adobo sauce with the cream cheese and set aside.

4. Now, assemble the lasagna. First grease the pan. Now add the lasagne noodles. Spread the chipotle sauce on top and then the salsa verde, and finally the black beans. Top with the cheddar cheese. Continue making these layers until you reach the last layer. Top the last layer with the chipotle sauce, salsa verde and cheddar cheese. Bake in the over for 35 minutes and then broil for 10 minutes on high until the cheese bubbles and turns golden brown.

5. Top the baked Mexican Lasagna with sliced red onion, avocado slices, lemon juice, and cilantro.

6. Serve the Mexican Lasagna with some chips and guacamole and passion fruit margaritas. Binge watching Monarca on Netflix is highly encouraged.

Roasted Poblano and Manchego Empanadas

I once had these incredible empanadas at Stanton Social, a Chris Santos restaurant in Manhattan. They were so flavorful and I knew I had to recreate these at home. These empanadas are the perfect party hors d'oeuvres and are surely to impress your guests. They are tiny flavor bombs and you will be so happy with the outcome. I highly recommend making these for your next cocktail party. Just be sure to make a lot because they go fast.

- ✐ Prep time 10 minutes
- ⏲ Cook time 50 minutes
- 🍴 Servings 6-8 servings
- 🕐 Total time 1 hour

INGREDIENTS

ROASTED POBLANO AND MANCHEGO EMPANADAS

- 4-5 poblano peppers, roasted
- 2 tablespoons extra-virgin olive oil
- 4 cloves of garlic, minced or crushed
- 2 shallots, diced
- ½ cup fresh chopped cilantro
- 2 tablespoons cumin powder
- 2 tablespoons taco seasoning
- Salt and black pepper to taste
- Butter to coat the empanadas before they bake
- 1 cup of shredded manchego cheese
- 1 11.6 oz. empanada discs (12 come in a pack)

CILANTRO LIME CREMA

- 1-2 cups cup fresh cilantro
- ½ cup of Greek yogurt
- 2 tablespoons cumin powder
- 2 tablespoons taco seasoning
- 2-3 cloves of garlic
- ½ jalapeño, de-seeded (optional)
- 1 tablespoon fresh squeezed lime juice
- Salt and black pepper to taste

INSTRUCTIONS

1. Pre-heat the oven to 425 degrees F.

2. De-seed the poblano peppers, coat them in olive oil and roast in the oven for 30 minutes until charred.

3. In a pan, on medium heat, sauté garlic in olive oil, until fragrant. Add in the diced shallots, cilantro, cumin powder, and taco seasoning. Cook for about 10 minutes. Add in the roasted poblano peppers and allow to cook for 10 more minutes. Take a hand blender and blend the mixture until a little chunky, not completely smooth. Add salt and black pepper to taste. Then fold in the shredded manchego cheese.

4. You can use the empanada dough discos or roll out puff pastry sheets and cut out 4 ½ inch rounds for the empanadas. Add some filling to the center of the round and line the edges with water. Then fold the puff pastry in half and take a fork and pressed down the edges. Continue the same process for all of the empanadas. Take some olive oil and coat the top of each empanada.

5. Adjust the temperature of the oven to 375 degrees F. Bake the empanadas for 15-20 minutes until a nice golden color is achieved.

6. In the meantime, for the Cilantro Lime Crema, blend together Greek yogurt, cumin powder, taco seasoning, garlic, jalapeño cilantro, and lemon juice with salt to taste.

7. Plate the empanadas and garnish them with some thinly sliced radishes with lime juice and salt and some cilantro and serve with the Cilantro Lime Crema.

8. Enjoy these empanadas hot with your favorite cocktail in hand.

Classic Italian Lasagna

This vegetarian lasagna has been a family staple for so long. I can make it with my eyes closed and the best part is that you can indulge in this lasagna almost guilt free because of all of the veggies I pack into it. It is the perfect meal to make on Christmas day or for any family gathering ("Merry Christmas ya filthy animal, and a Happy New Year"). It can be made ahead of time and baked when ready too. Added bonus for any picky eaters who happen to be kids, or vegetable challenged adults-there are so many veggies in this lasagna that get blended into a mixture that no one can tell. Serve it with some delicious Italian garlic bread and enjoy with a glass of red wine. Also, binging The Godfather is highly encouraged. And remember, "Drop the gun, leave the cannoli." Is it a guy thing to always quote The Godfather?

- ✎ Prep time 15 minutes
- ◔ Cook time 45 minutes
- 🍴 Servings 6 servings
- 🕐 Total time 1 hour

Mansi Akruwala

INGREDIENTS

CLASSIC ITALIAN LASAGNA

- 1 box of 9 oz. oven-ready lasagne noodles
- 1 2 lb. part skim ricotta cheese
- 1 zucchini, shredded
- 1 8 oz. part skim shredded mozzarella cheese
- Fresh pre-sliced mozzarella
- 1 8 oz. bag of baby spinach
- 1 medium sized onion, finely diced.
- 1 cup fresh basil, chopped
- 4-5 cloves of garlic, minced or crushed
- ½ cup pesto, homemade or store bought
- 1 tablespoon calabrian chili sauce
- 2 tablespoons Italian seasoning or sofritos seasoning (dried oregano and basil, garlic powder, etc.)
- Salt and pepper to taste

HOMEMADE MARINARA SAUCE

- 1 28 OZ. CAN OF SAN MARZANO TOMATOES
- ¼ CUP EXTRA-VIRGIN OLIVE OIL
- 3-4 CLOVES OF GARLIC, CRUSHED OR MINCED
- 2 TABLESPOONS DRIED OREGANO
- ½ CUP FRESH CHOPPED BASIL, AND MORE FOR GARNISH
- 2 TABLESPOONS CALABRIAN CHILI SAUCE
- SALT AND BLACK PEPPER TO TASTE

THE BEST GARLIC BREAD

- 1 ITALIAN BREAD LOAF
- BUTTER
- EXTRA-VIRGIN OLIVE OIL
- DRIED OREGANO
- PARMESAN CHEESE, SHREDDED
- SALT AND BLACK PEPPER TO TASTE

INSTRUCTIONS

1. Pre-heat the oven to 375 degrees F.

2. Sauté the garlic and onions in olive oil, until fragrant. Add in the fresh chopped basil, and Italian seasoning. Cook for 10 minutes. Add in the spinach, pesto, and shredded zucchini. Cook for 10 minutes and then add in the ricotta cheese and stir well. Cook for another 10 minutes. Then take a hand blender and blend the mixture until smooth. The spinach and ricotta mixture should be a pretty green color.

3. Make the Homemade Marinara Sauce. In a pan, on medium heat, sauté garlic in olive oil, until fragrant. Add in the dried oregano, chopped basil, and Calabrian chilis. Next, add in the San Marzano tomatoes. Cook and simmer the sauce for at least 25 to 30 minutes, allowing the flavors to develop and the tomatoes to break down. Sauce can be left chunky or my personal preference is to take a hand blender and blend slightly. Add salt and black pepper to taste.

4. Slice the Italian bread and make a mixture of melted butter and olive oil, dried oregano, and salt and pepper to taste. Toast in the oven on 375 degrees F for about 6-7 minutes or until golden and crispy.

5. Time to layer the lasagna. In a baking pan, layer the bottom with sauce first, and then arrange the lasagna noodles next to one another. Top with the spinach and ricotta mixture and then layer it with the marinara sauce. Add fresh chopped basil and shredded mozzarella. Continue making these layers, about 3 should suffice. For the final layer. Place the lasagne noodles first, and then layer down the marinara sauce and top with a combination of fresh and processed shredded mozzarella cheese.

6. Bake for 30 minutes in the oven while covered with aluminum foil. For the final 10-15 minutes, bake on broil until a lovely gold color is achieved and the cheese is bubbling. Top with fresh chopped basil and some grated parmesan cheese.

7. Serve a big heaping portion with some delicious crusty garlic bread and a nice glass of red wine.

Spicy Rigatoni Alla Vodka

I am not sure why, but I associate Rigatoni Alla Vodka with every mom and pop Italian restaurant on Long Island, where I was born and raised. Of course, I also associate good deli egg and cheese sandwiches, the best bagels, and Italian rainbow cookies with Long Island as well. However, there is something so nostalgic about this dish and I prefer to make it on a cold, snowy night, it really sets the mood. Around Christmas is the perfect time for this pasta. It is one of my most favorite Italian dishes and is really so simple. My Rigatoni Alla Vodka is a little different because I add some heat and I finish it with fresh torn basil and creamy burrata, which truly is the cherry on the top. Also, here comes the surprise-there is no vodka in it! This is just one of those creamy, satisfying, heart-warming recipes that is meant to be made in bulk and enjoyed with your family, regardless of the occasion. Also, does anyone else listen to Sinatra when they cook Italian food? Anybody? No? Just me? Ok, then…

- ✎ Prep time 10 minutes
- ⏱ Cook time 30 minutes
- 🍴 Servings 8-10 servings
- 🕐 Total time 45 minutes

INGREDIENTS

RIGATONI ALLA VODKA

- 1 16 oz. box of rigatoni pasta
- 1 6 oz can of tomato paste
- 2 pints of heavy cream
- 4 cloves of garlic, minced or crushed
- 2 tablespoons extra-virgin olive oil
- 2 tablespoons of calabrian chili sauce or crushed red pepper flakes
- Creamy burrata cheese
- Fresh chopped basil
- Grated parmesan cheese

INSTRUCTIONS

1. Boil the rigatoni pasta, about 8-10 minutes for al dente.

2. In a pan on medium heat, sauté the garlic in olive oil until fragrant and then add the tomato paste and Calabrian chilis or crushed red pepper flakes. Once everything has cooked for 5 minutes, add the heavy cream, and mix with a whisk. Allow the sauce to simmer on medium for 15-20 minutes, allowing the flavors to merry and build.

3. Mix in the cooked pasta into the sauce. Top with shredded parmesan cheese, chopped fresh basil, and creamy burrata.

4. Serve yourself and your family a big bowl of the Spicy Rigatoni Alla Vodka and put on Home Alone 1 and 2.

5. Enjoy "ya filthy animals".

Mansi Akruwala

Truffle Mushroom Pasta

This pasta is for truffle lovers. It is so decadent and creamy that it will have you reaching for seconds, and maybe even thirds. Truffle and mushrooms are a marriage made in culinary heaven and this cream sauce is finger-licking good.

- Prep time 5 minutes
- Cook time 45 minutes
- Servings 6 servings
- Total time 1 hour

INGREDIENTS

TRUFFLE MUSHROOM PASTA

- 1 1 16 oz. box of bow-tie or farfalle pasta
- 1 pint heavy cream
- Truffle salt
- 1 8 oz. of baby bella mushrooms, sliced
- 4 cloves of garlic, minced or crushed
- 2 shallots, diced
- 1 cup fresh chopped basil and more to garnish with
- 2 tablespoons Italian seasoning
- 1 sprig of fresh rosemary
- 2 sprigs of fresh thyme

INSTRUCTIONS

1. Boil the farfalle pasta to al dente, follow instructions on box, but usually 10-12 minutes.

2. Sauté the garlic and shallots in olive oil, until fragrant. Add in the chopped fresh basil, rosemary, thyme and Italian seasoning. Add in the sliced baby bella mushrooms. Cook for 15 minutes until soft and tender. Then add the heavy cream and the truffle salt. Cook for another 15 minutes, bringing the sauce to a simmer.

3. Add in the cooked pasta, top with fresh basil and serve with a glass of red wine.

Baked Feta Pasta

I got a story to tell...I actually I don't BUT when I was making this pasta I was listening to Biggie, one of my favorite artists and truly the GOAT of Hip Hop, and dare I say music in general. His lyrical story telling was ingenious, and his flow and delivery was visceral. Although I cannot personally relate to his lyrics, I can say that his music transports me to his childhood and upbringing on the street corners of Brooklyn. I instantly feel a wide range of emotions from his music and his ability to tell a story so poetically. I highly recommend the documentary, "Biggie: I Got a Story to Tell" on Netflix-an incredible documentary about his life and raw testimonials from his friends and family, including none other than Puffy himself. Anyways, I digress! Back to food. This is the pasta that was all the craze on tik tok and Instagram. I must have seen a hundred of these videos being posted, and all them had variations in their recipe. This pasta is easy and delicious and well it is a must make item for any social media crazy millennial.

Mansi Akruwala

/ Prep time 5 minutes

◉ Cook time 45 minutes

⑂ Servings 6 servings

◷ Total time 1 hour

INGREDIENTS

BAKED FETA PASTA

- 1 1 16 oz. box of bow-tie or farfalle pasta
- 1 slab of fresh feta cheese
- ¼ cup extra-virgin olive oil
- 3-4 cups of chopped fresh baby spinach
- 1 pint of cherry or grape tomatoes, halved
- 1/2 cup of sundried tomatoes, halved
- 8 cloves of garlic, whole
- 2 shallots, sliced
- 1 cup fresh chopped basil and more to garnish with
- 2 tablespoons Italian seasoning
- 1 sprig of fresh rosemary
- 2 sprigs of fresh thyme

INSTRUCTIONS

1. Pre-heat the oven to 375 degrees F.

2. Boil the farfalle pasta to al dente, follow instructions on box, but usually 10-12 minutes.

3. In a baking pan, add the feta block with the tomatoes, sliced shallots, sun-dried tomatoes, and whole garlic. Add in the olive oil, Italian seasoning, rosemary and thyme. Bake for 45 minutes, you can broil for the last 10 minutes to achieve a golden color on the feta. The vegetables will all be caramelized and fill your kitchen with wonderful aromas.

4. Add in the cooked farfalle, chopped baby spinach, and fresh basil to the baked feta dish. Give it a good mix and serve hot.

5. Enjoy this pasta and make sure to post a video to Instagram or tik tok.

Ricotta and Pesto Gnocchi in Ancho Chili Sauce

One of the things I love about cooking is being able to experiment with different flavors and ingredients. I get to be a scientist in the kitchen, perfecting recipes through trial error and using my willing family members as guinea pigs. This pasta recipe was in fact invented in my very own kitchen and it is probably one of my most favorite recipes. The gnocchi are little bites of fluffy, airy pillows, cloud-like almost and the sauce is so creamy, with slight heat and simply divine. Do not let the title of this dish scare you away. While this recipe does include both ancho chili powder and calabrian chili sauce, it is not actually spicy. And both can be adjusted for desired spice level.

- ✑ Prep time 25 minutes
- ⧖ Cook time 30 minutes
- 🍴 Servings 6 servings
- ⏱ Total time 55 minutes

Mansi Akruwala

INGREDIENTS

RICOTTA AND PESTO GNOCCHI

- 1 cup all purpose flour
- 1 ½ cup whole milk ricotta
- ¼ cup homemade or store bought pesto
- 3 egg yolks
- ½ cup parmesan cheese, shredded
- 2 tablespoons black pepper
- Salt to taste

ANCHO CHILI SAUCE

- 1 pint of heavy cream
- 1 tablespoon extra virgin olive oil
- 4 cloves of garlic, minced or crushed
- 1 tablespoon ancho chili powder, adjust for desired spice level
- 1 tablespoon calabrian chili sauce, adjust for desired spice level
- 2 tablespoons sofritos seasoning or any Italian seasoning mix
- 3 tablespoons fresh basil, chiffonade cut
- 2 shallots
- 2 tablespoons cornstarch

CRISPY SAGE AND BASIL PARMESAN PANKO BREADCRUMBS

- 1 cup panko breadcrumbs
- 1-2 tablespoons unsalted butter
- 1 tablespoon extra virgin olive oil
- ½ cup fresh basil, chiffonade cut
- ½ cup fresh sage, chiffonade cut
- ½ cup parmesan cheese, shredded
- Sea salt or Maldon sea salt flakes for finishing

INSTRUCTIONS

1. Bring a large pot of salted water to a boil over high heat.

2. Add the egg yolks to the ricotta and stir briefly to combine. Add in the flour, parmesan, salt and pepper, and stir until evenly combined. The dough should be moist and a bit sticky, but it should be holding together well. If it feels too wet, just add in another few tablespoons of flour.

3. Roll out and cut the dough. Take the dough in small portions and transfer it to a lightly-floured cutting board and sprinkle the dough with flour. This will make the dough easy to work with. Roll out thin logs of the dough. Cut each log into individual bite-sized little gnocchi squares or pillows. Give the gnocchi a quick toss so that they are all lightly coated with flour. This will help prevent them from sticking together.

4. Boil the gnocchi. Carefully transfer the gnocchi to the boiling water to cook. Then once they float — usually after 30 seconds or so — drain the gnocchi.

5. In a pan on medium heat, sauté the garlic in olive oil until fragrant. Add in the chiffonade basil and then the ancho chili powder and the calabrian chili sauce. Mix together and allow to cook for 5 minutes. Next, add in the heavy cream. Allow the sauce to come to a boil and then simmer for 12-15 minutes. Finish with salt to taste.

6. In a pan on medium heat, sauté the garlic in olive oil and butter, add in the panko breadcrumbs, basil, and sage. Stir to combine and cook for 3 minutes. Then add the shredded parmesan and mix it all together. Cook for another 3 minutes. The breadcrumbs should be crispy and golden and they should be held together by the melted parmesan cheese. Finish with light sea salt.

7. Now plate the gnocchi and pour the sauce on top. Then top with the Crispy Sage and Basil Parmesan Panko Breadcrumbs.

Greek Orzo Salad

One of the most wonderful things about traveling is being able to explore the local cuisine. In fact, I draw a lot of my recipe inspiration from my travels. In 2015, I was fortunate enough to be invited to my dear friend, Deena's wedding in Corfu, Greece. It was her #bigfatGreekEgyptian wedding and I got to enjoy a week with my closest college friends, and we had a blast. Deena is a fellow foodie and phenomenal cook so it was a no brainer that her wedding would also include incredible food. I got the opportunity to visit a beautiful island with stunning blue water and the kindest people, and of course mouth-watering local food. Everything from the spanakopita, to the fresh Greek salads, and frappes to the baklavas were all simply magnificent. I could not get over how fresh and incredibly tasty the local produce was. The tomatoes were so red, I thought they must have been colored red! This Greek Orzo Salad was made to recreate some of the flavors that I got to indulge in during my time in Corfu. I swear every bite takes me back to Barbati beach. Enjoy this salad on a summer day spent by the pool with unlimited iced teas. Also, as I type this I am currently on Expedia, "booking" aka daydreaming about my next vacation to Greece.

- ✎ Prep time 10 minutes
- ⏱ Cook time 15 minutes
- 🍴 Servings 6 servings
- 🕐 Total time 25 minutes

Mansi Akruwala

INGREDIENTS

GREEK ORZO SALAD

- 8 oz. of dry orzo
- 2-3 cups of chopped baby spinach
- 1 cup of cherry tomatoes, halved
- ½ cup English cucumbers, diced into small cubes
- ½ cup kalamata olives, halved
- ¼ cup extra-virgin (Greek) olive oil
- ½ cup sun-dried tomatoes
- ½ cup chopped fresh basil
- Tzatziki seasoning (Alternatively, you can make your own mix with garlic powder, dried dill, rosemary, oregano, basil, salt and pepper to taste)
- ½ cup cubed feta cheese

INSTRUCTIONS

1. Cook the orzo in salted, boiling water, for about 10 minutes.

2. Then add in the chopped spinach, tomatoes, cucumbers, kalamata olives, basil, sun-dried tomatoes, Tzatziki seasoning, and crumbled feta. Finish with the olive oil and salt and pepper to taste. Mix everything together.

3. Enjoy the Greek Orzo Salad on a hot summer day.

Mansi Akruwala

Grilled Halloumi and Garlic Asparagus

This is the perfect meal to go with a nice cabernet, one of my favorite wines. This dish was also influenced by my travels to Corfu, Greece. I love how simple and easy it is and how pretty it looks when it is plated. This dish is effortless, but so chic and screams high dining. The salty and stringy bite of the Grilled Halloumi cheese pairs perfectly with the Roasted Asparagus with garlic. The char marks are a must on both the Halloumi and the asparagus. Create the perfect date night with this dish, light some candles, and enjoy with your partner.

- ✎ Prep time 5 minutes
- ⏱ Cook time 10-15 minutes
- 🍴 Servings 4 servings
- 🕐 Total time 30 minutes

INGREDIENTS

GRILLED HALLOUMI AND ROASTED ASPARAGUS

- 1 slab of Halloumi cheese
- 1 bunch of asparagus
- 3-4 cloves of garlic, minced or crushed, or sliced is fine too
- 2 tablespoons extra-virgin olive oil
- Sea salt and black pepper to taste

INSTRUCTIONS

1. Pre-heat the oven to 400 degrees F.

2. Wash and chop the stems off of the asparagus. Toss the asparagus with the olive oil, sea salt, and black pepper. Place on a baking sheet and roast in the oven for about 10-15 minutes, until golden brown and crispy.

3. In a pan, on medium heat, in some olive oil, grill the halloumi cheese until golden brown, about 5 to 7 minutes

Fall Roasted Butternut Squash Arugula Salad with Goat Cheese

Have I mentioned how much I love roasted butternut squash? I have two recipes in this cookbook, all featuring butternut squash so you do the math. This is the perfect salad in the Fall and my favorite to make during Thanksgiving. Roasted butternut squash is incredibly flavorful, nutty, and crispy, and pairs so well with the peppery arugula, the creamy goat cheese, and the tart and slightly sweet balsamic vinaigrette.

- ✎ Prep time 5 minutes
- ◔ Cook time 45 minutes
- 🍴 Servings 6-8 servings
- 🕐 Total time 30 minutes

INGREDIENTS

ROASTED BUTTERNUT SQUASH TACOS

- 1 15 oz. pre-cut butternut squash cubes
- 2 tablespoons extra-virgin olive oil
- Salt and black pepper to taste
- 1 5 oz. goat cheese log, crumbled
- 1 5 oz. bag of arugula salad
- Balsamic vinegar and extra-virgin olive oil
- Pecans, slivered

INSTRUCTIONS

1. Pre-heat the oven to 425 degrees F.

2. Toss the butternut squash in the olive oil, salt, and black pepper. Place on a baking sheet and roasted the butternut squash for 45 minutes in the oven, until crispy and charred.

3. For the balsamic vinaigrette, mix balsamic vinegar with olive oil, salt, and pepper, and some crumbled goat cheese. Whisk until the dressing has emulsified and is creamy.

4. Toss the arugula salad with the cooled butternut squash and top with slivered pecans, and crumbled goat cheese.

Roasted Sweet Potato Fries With Cilantro Lime Crema

I love bar food. In fact, I look forward to going to a bar, not for the drinks, but for the food. Bring on all of the nachos, truffle fries, jalapeno poppers, and mozzarella sticks. The cheesier the better. French fries can be an incredibly satisfying and delicious bar food stable. It is one of my favorite things to eat with a cold beer. These Roasted Sweet Potato Fries are so delicious, and the cooling Cilantro Lime Crema is perfect with them. Grab a cold beer and sit back and watch the basketball game. Steph Curry fans are always welcome.

- Prep time 10 minutes
- Cook time 45 minutes
- Servings 4 servings
- Total time 1 hour

Mansi Akruwala

INGREDIENTS

ROASTED SWEET POTATO FRIES

- 3-4 sweet potatoes, sliced into wedges
- 3-4 cloves of garlic, minced or crushed
- ½ cup of parmesan cheese, shredded
- ¼ cup of extra-virgin olive oil
- 1 tablespoon of Cayenne pepper, add extra for more heat
- Salt and black pepper to taste
- Cilantro, to garnish

CILANTRO LIME CREMA

- 1-2 cups cup fresh cilantro
- ½ cup of Greek yogurt
- 2 tablespoons cumin powder
- 2 tablespoons taco seasoning
- 2-3 cloves of garlic
- ½ jalapeño, de-seeded (optional)
- 1 tablespoon fresh squeezed lime juice
- Salt and black pepper to taste

INSTRUCTIONS

1. Pre-heat the oven to 375 degrees F.

2. After peeling and dicing the sweet potatoes into wedges, add olive oil, crushed garlic, cayenne pepper, salt and black pepper. Toss to coat the mixture evenly.

3. On a baking sheet, spread out the sweet potato fries and bake or air-fry them for 45 minutes. You can add the shredded parmesan cheese during the last 10 minutes of baking, until it melts a bit.

4. For the crema, blend together cilantro, lime juice, jalapeño, cumin powder, taco seasoning, Greek yogurt, garlic, and salt and black pepper to taste.

Crispy Tofu with Spicy Peanut Sauce and Grilled Garlic Broccolini

This meal is Asian inspired, and I love it because it really is so easy to make and prepare ahead of time, especially the Spicy Peanut Sauce, which can be made and stored ahead of time.

- Prep time 10 minutes
- Cook time 30 minutes
- Servings 4 servings
- Total time 1 hour

Mansi Akruwala

INGREDIENTS

CRISPY TOFU

- 1 14 oz. extra firm tofu
- ½ cup rice flour
- ½ cup chickpea flour or besan
- Water
- 2 cups panko breadcrumbs
- 2 tablespoons garlic powder
- Salt to taste
- Cooking spray

SPICY PEANUT SAUCE

- ½ CUP OF PEANUT BUTTER
- 2 TABLESPOONS OLIVE OIL
- 2 TABLESPOONS SIRACHA
- 3-4 CLOVES OF GARLIC
- ½ CUP CILANTRO, CHOPPED
- 1 TABLESPOON RICE WINE VINEGAR
- 2 TABLESPOONS FRESH SQUEEZED LIME JUICE
- 2 TABLESPOONS HONEY
- WATER TO MAKE SAUCE MORE LIQUID

GRILLED GARLIC BROCCOLINI

- BROCCOLINI
- 3-4 CLOVES OF GARLIC, MINCED OR CRUSHED
- 1 TABLESPOON SESAME OIL
- 1 TABLESPOON EXTRA-VIRGIN OLIVE OIL
- 2 TABLESPOONS SOY SAUCE

INSTRUCTIONS

1. Pre-heat the oven to 425 degrees F.

2. For the dressing, in a blender, combine peanut butter, olive oil, Siracha, garlic, cilantro, rice wine vinegar, lime juice, honey, and blend. Add water as needed for desired creamy dressing consistency.

3. Coat the tofu block in the Spicy Peanut Sauce marinade.

4. On a hot grill, grill the tofu on both sides. Char it nicely and set aside.

5. In the same hot grill, add sesame oil and olive oil and sauté garlic, until fragrant. Add in the broccolini with the soy sauce and cook for 10 to 15 minutes until tender.

6. Serve the tofu on a dish with the Spicy Peanut Sauce and the Grilled Garlic Broccolini.

Shiitake Steamed Buns

One of the best things I ever ate were the Shiitake Steamed Buns at Momofuku Noodle Bar in the East Village, a David Chang restaurant. The mushrooms were so incredibly flavorful, and the pickled cucumbers and scallions were the perfect refreshing crisp bite to contrast them and together inside a soft steamed lotus bun. The umami flavor that David Chang managed to develop in this dish is worth every praise and honor. These of course are my own take on them, so the recipe is different than what you would find at Momofuku, but I promise they are just as delicious. These buns will have even the devout of mushroom skeptics believing. Pair these buns with a crisp shredded broccoli and kale salad with a Spicy Creamy Peanut Dressing, and I promise you will be in culinary heaven. Tonight's meal will be featuring David Chang's travelogue, "Ugly Delicious" on Netflix, where David explores culinary hotspots around the world, including pizza, tacos, and fried chicken.

- 🔪 Prep time 10 minutes
- 🍳 Cook time 35 minutes
- 🍴 Servings 4 servings
- 🕐 Total time 50 minutes

Mansi Akruwala

INGREDIENTS

Shiitake Steamed Buns

- 1 package of shiitake mushrooms, sliced
- 2 tablespoons sesame oil
- 1 tablespoon extra-virgin olive oil
- 2-3 cloves of garlic, minced or crushed
- 1 teaspoon siracha sauce
- 2 tablespoons hoisin sauce
- 1 tablespoon soy sauce
- 1 tablespoon liquid smoke
- 1/2 cup of water
- Scallions, finely chopped
- Lotus buns, found in the Asian grocery store in the frozen section

Pickled Cucumbers

- 1 Persian seedless cucumber, very thinly sliced
- 1 teaspoon sugar
- 1 teaspoon salt
- ½ cup of ice-cold water
- 2 tablespoons rice wine vinegar or mirin (mirin is a good alternative; however, it is sweeter and has alcohol in it)

INSTRUCTIONS

1. In a pan on medium heat, sauté the garlic in the olive oil and sesame oil until fragrant. Next add the shiitake mushrooms. Cook them until tender and then continue to cook until crispy, about 20 minutes. Add in the soy sauce, hoisin, siracha, liquid smoke, and water. Continue to cook for another 5-7 minutes.

2. Steam the lotus buns for 2-3 minutes. Alternatively, you can wrap them in a wet paper towel in the microwave for 30-45 seconds.

3. In the meantime, pickle the cucumbers. Add the thinly sliced cucumbers to cold water with salt, sugar, and rice wine vinegar. Let sit for at least 15 to 20 minutes. The longer, the more pickled the cucumbers will get.

4. After the lotus buns have been steamed, add the shiitake mushroom mixture, then the pickled cucumbers and chopped scallions.

5. Enjoy with a delicious and crisp shredded broccoli and kale salad with spicy creamy peanut sauce.

Crunchy Asian Salad

There is nothing I love more than a good salad and a great dressing. This Asian salad is incredibly easy and delicious. Enjoy with the Shiitake Steamed Buns or with some ramen. It is the perfect healthy meal and I hope you enjoy it.

- ✎ Prep time 5 minutes
- ☻ Cook time 10 minutes
- ⍨ Servings 4 servings
- ◷ Total time 15 minutes

INGREDIENTS

CRUNCHY ASIAN SALAD

- 1 bag broccoli and kale slaw salad mix (Found at Trader Joe's)
- ½ cup scallions, finely chopped
- ½ cup unsalted peanuts, chopped,
- Fresh cilantro to garnish
- 1 package extra firm tofu, diced into cubes

Spicy Peanut Dressing

- ½ CUP OF PEANUT BUTTER (CASHEW BUTTER WOULD ALSO WORK WELL)
- 2 TABLESPOONS OLIVE OIL
- 2 TABLESPOONS SIRACHA
- 3-4 CLOVES OF GARLIC
- ½ CUP CILANTRO, CHOPPED
- 1 TABLESPOON RICE WINE VINEGAR
- 2 TABLESPOONS FRESH SQUEEZED LIME JUICE
- 2 TABLESPOONS HONEY
- WATER TO MAKE SAUCE MORE LIQUID

INSTRUCTIONS

1. For the dressing, in a blender, combine peanut butter, olive oil, Siracha, garlic, cilantro, rice wine vinegar, lime juice, honey, and blend. Add water as needed for desired creamy dressing consistency.

2. Add the bag of broccoli and kale slaw salad mix to a big salad bowl. Top with chopped scallions and cilantro. Toss in the tofu, and drizzle the Spicy Peanut Dressing on top. Serve and enjoy, guilt free.

Veggie Steamed Dumplings

Veggie Steamed Dumplings are the perfect nutritious and umami meal to make for a date night or for a night in with friends, playing poker and perhaps watching old Bruce Lee films on Netflix. The Ip Man movies are actually a personal favorite for something more recent. Enjoy these Veggie Steamed Dumplings served warm.

- ✐ Prep time 15 minutes
- ⏱ Cook time 45 minutes
- 🍴 Servings 4 servings
- ⏱ Total time 1 hour

INGREDIENTS

Veggie Steamed Dumplings

- 1 8 oz. package of shiitake mushrooms, sliced
- 1 12 oz. package of wonton wrappers
- 2-3 carrots, shredded
- 2-3 cups of chopped fresh baby spinach
- 3 shallots, diced
- 4 cloves of garlic, minced or crushed
- 2 teaspoons fresh grated ginger
- 2 tablespoons extra virgin olive oil
- 2 tablespoons hoisin sauce
- 2 tablespoons soy sauce
- 2 tablespoons sesame oil
- 1 tablespoon chili garlic sauce or siracha
- 1 tablespoon miso paste
- ½ cup scallions, finely chopped

Dipping Sauce

- 2 tablespoons soy sauce
- 1 tablespoon white wine vinegar or mirin
- 1 teaspoon siracha
- 1 tablespoon honey
- Sesame seeds
- 1 squeeze of lime juice

INSTRUCTIONS

1. Sauté the garlic and ginger in olive oil over medium heat, until fragrant. Add in the diced shallots, mushrooms, carrots, and chopped baby spinach. Cook for 10-15 minutes until mushrooms are soft and tender. Add in the hoisin, soy sauce, sesame oil, chili garlic sauce or siracha, and miso paste. Cook for another 10 minutes. Add in chopped scallions and mix together to form the filling for the wontons.

2. In the meantime, combine the hoisin, soy sauce, siracha, white wine vinegar or mirin, honey, and lime for a quick but delicious dipping sauce.

3. Fill the wonton wrappers. Spoon in the filling onto the water and seal the edges with water. Pinching in the opposite 4 corners to form the dumpling.

4. You can use a bamboo steamer or simply boil water in a pot and put a metal colander with holes in it, on top of the boiling water pot. Place the dumplings in the colander and steam for about 10 minutes. Dumplings should be soft and transparent when done. Coat with more finely chopped scallions and sesame seeds.

5. Serve the dumplings warm with the dipping sauce and put on your favorite Kung Fu movie.

Indochinese Hakka Noodles

Indian-Chinese or Indochinese food is one of my favorite cuisines. It combines the flavors of two cultures rich in flavor. This recipe is super quick and delicious and so satisfying. It is packed with big bold flavors and a healthy dinner meal. Enjoy!

✎ Prep time 10 minutes
◉ Cook time 20 minutes
🍴 Servings 4 servings
🕐 Total time 30 minutes

INGREDIENTS

INDOCHINESE HAKKA NOODLES

- 1 package of hakka noodles
- 1 tablespoon canola oil
- 4 cloves garlic
- 1 teaspoon shredded ginger
- 1 red bell pepper, sliced
- 1 small head of broccoli
- 1 package shiitake mushrooms, sliced
- 2 shallots, sliced
- 3 tablespoons soy sauce
- 2 tablespoons hoisin sauce
- 3 tablespoons Hot and Spicy Maggi Sauce
- 2 tablespoons Manchurian seasoning
- 2 tablespoons Tandoori masala
- 1 tablespoon Siracha sauce
- 1 package extra firm tofu
- Cilantro and scallions to garnish

INSTRUCTIONS

1. In a medium wok style pan, sauté the garlic and ginger in some oil, until fragrant. Add in the shallots and red bell peppers and cook for 7-8 minutes until softened. Add the tofu, shiitake mushrooms, and broccoli and cook for another 12-15 minutes. Add in soy sauce, hoisin, Siracha, Maggi sauce, and water to thin out. Add In the Manchurian seasoning and tandoori masala. Stir and cook for another 5 minutes.

2. In the meantime, boil the hakka noodles as per package instructions.

3. Combine the cooked hakka noodles with the sautéed veggies and sauce.

4. Serve the Hakka noodles and enjoy!

White Miso, Tahini, and Red Curry Veggie Ramen

Recently, I attempted to make Meera Sodha's White Miso Ramen, and I was so impressed. The umami flavors that I developed were incredible and had me licking the bowl. Not the most appealing visual, but I will say her recipe was easy, and so delicious. I decided to make my own version, which is of course inspired by her. I use coconut cream and Thai red curry paste to give it a Thai twist. The tahini is absolutely delicious in this and enhances the flavor of the rich and bold broth. In fact, I often use Tahini in many of my Asian recipes because it evokes or even enhances the flavors of miso. This is the recipe you make on a cold night, and eat it on your couch with a cozy blanket and a great movie. This ramen is sure to warm your heart and soul. Thank you for the inspiration, Meera.

- ✐ Prep time 15 minutes
- ◔ Cook time 25 minutes
- 🍴 Servings 4 servings
- 🕐 Total time 1 hour

INGREDIENTS

WHITE MISO AND TAHINI VEGGIE RAMEN

- 1 PACKAGE OF SHIITAKE MUSHROOMS, SLICED
- 1 TABLESPOON TAHINI PASTE
- 2 TABLESPOONS SOY SAUCE
- 4 CLOVES OF GARLIC
- 2 TEASPOONS GINGER
- 1 SHALLOT
- 2 TABLESPOONS CHILI GARLIC SAUCE, ADJUST FOR SPICE LEVEL
- 1 TABLESPOON WHITE MISO PASTE
- 2 TABLESPOONS THAI RED CURRY PASTE
- 2 CUPS OF LIGHT COCONUT CREAM OR MILK
- 1 TABLESPOON RED CURRY PASTE
- WATER, TO THIN OUT BROTH
- 8 SOFT-BOILED EGGS
- 1 PACKAGE RAMEN NOODLES
- SLICED GREEN ONIONS FOR GARNISH
- SESAME SEEDS FOR GARNISH
- CHILI GARLIC SAUCE FOR GARNISH

CRISPY EDAMAME

- 2 cups edamame, shelled and whole
- 3 CLOVES OF GARLIC
- 1 TABLESPOON SESAME OIL
- 1 TABLESPOON SOY SAUCE
- 1-2 TABLESPOONS CHILI GARLIC SAUCE
- 1-2 SQUEEZES OF LEMON JUICE

Sautéed Baby Bok Choy

- 1 package baby bok choy, whole
- 3 cloves of garlic
- 1 tablespoon sesame oil
- 1 tablespoon soy sauce
- 1-2 tablespoons chili garlic sauce

Sautéed Garlic Broccolini

- 1 package of broccolini, chopped
- 3 cloves of garlic
- 1 tablespoon sesame oil
- 1 tablespoon soy sauce
- 1-2 tablespoons chili garlic sauce

Crispy Shiitake Mushrooms

- 1 package of shiitake mushrooms, sliced
- 3 cloves of garlic
- 1 tablespoon sesame oil
- 1 tablespoon soy sauce
- 1 tablespoon hoisin
- 1-2 tablespoon chili garlic sauce

Crispy Tofu

- 1 package firm tofu, cubed
- 3-4 tablespoons corn starch
- 2 tablespoons hoisin sauce
- 2 tablespoons soy sauce
- 1-2 tablespoons chili garlic sauce
- Water to thin out

Crispy Fried Shallots

- 2 shallots, sliced
- 3-4 tablespoons cornstarch
- Salt to taste

INSTRUCTIONS

1. Pre-heat the oven or air fryer to 425 degrees F.

2. Put the shiitake mushrooms in a heatproof bowl, cover with just-boiled water and leave to soak for five minutes.

3. Take the cubed tofu and toss and coat in cornstarch. Spray a non-stick baking sheet and bake the tofu for 20 minutes, until crispy. When tofu is baked and crispy add in the soy sauce, hoisin, chili garlic sauce, and water to thin out. Toss the sauce mixture with the tofu and set aside.

4. In a pan on medium heat, add sesame oil, sauté garlic, shallots, and ginger, until fragrant. Add the chili garlic sauce, and soy sauce. Mix and then add the soaked mushrooms with some of the water they were soaking in. Let cook for 10 minutes. Then blend together to make the broth. Add water to thin out.

5. Place broth mixture in a pot and turn on heat to medium. Add in the tahini, miso paste, and coconut cream or milk. Stir and cook for 10 minutes, bringing to a boil and then lowering heat to simmer.

6. Next, cook the noodles to the packet instructions, drain, rinse under cold water and drain again.

7. Heat sesame oil in a pan and add in garlic until fragrant and then add in edamame. Add in the soy sauce, chili garlic sauce, and cook until crispy and brown. Add in a squeeze of fresh lemon juice. Set aside.

8. In the same pan, again add sesame oil, and then sauté garlic until fragrant. Add in the bok choy, soy sauce and chili garlic. Cook for 7 minutes until the bok choy browns and gets a little crispy. Set aside.

9. Next, in a pan heat another tablespoon of sesame oil, sauté the garlic until fragrant then add in the mushrooms. Cook for 5 minutes. Add in the soy sauce, hoisin, and chili garlic sauce. Cook for another 7 minutes until crispy. Set aside.

10. For the crispy shallots, toss sliced shallots into a bowl mixed with cornstarch. Shallow fry in 1-2 inches of oil, until golden brown and crispy. Sprinkle some salt on them when done. Set aside.

11. Prepare 8 soft boiled eggs. Boil for 6 to 8 minutes for desired softness. Yolk should be softened to gel-like.

12. Now assemble the Ramen bowls. To assemble, divide the noodles between four bowls. Reheat the miso and tahini broth, if you need to, and share among the bowls. Lay some tofu to one side of each bowl, and add the soft-boiled eggs cut in half. Add the broccolini, crispy mushrooms, bok choy and edamame beans evenly, and serve hot. Then add the scallions and crispy shallots. Finally, finish off with some chili garlic sauce and sesame seeds for garnish.

13. Serve and enjoy with a cozy blanket and movie.

Roasted Purple Sweet Potatoes With A Spicy Creamy Cashew Cream

Recently, I have been trying to incorporate more plant-based meals into my diet and lifestyle. Mostly because plant-based diets are what are strongly encouraged by the American Heart Association. Plant-based diets are associated with reduced heart disease risk because they are typically not high in cholesterol and saturated fats. And to be quite frank, I could benefit from a little less cheese in my life. This dish is so easy to make and so flavorful you will not miss the cheese, fat, or meat. Additionally, it is very aesthetically pleasing, and the rich purple color of the sweet potatoes are so inviting.

- Prep time 10 minutes
- Cook time 45 minutes
- Servings 4 servings
- Total time 1 hour

Mansi Akruwala

INGREDIENTS

ROASTED PURPLE SWEET POTATOES

- 3-4 purple sweet potatoes, chopped into cubes
- Salt and black pepper
- ¼ cup extra-virgin olive oil
- Sunflower seeds, to garnish
- Fresh cilantro, to garnish

CREAMY SPICY CASHEW CREAM

- 1 CUP CASHEWS, BOILED
- ½ CUP SALSA
- 3-4 CLOVES OF GARLIC
- 1 SHALLOT, SLICED
- 1 CUP FRESH CILANTRO
- 3-4 TABLESPOONS OF NUTRITIONAL YEAST
- ½ JALAPEÑO, DE-SEEDED (OPTIONAL)
- SALT AND BLACK PEPPER TO TASTE
- WATER

INSTRUCTIONS

1. Pre-heat the oven to 375 degrees F.

2. Chop the purple sweet potatoes and place on a baking sheet. Toss the sweet potatoes with olive oil, salt and black pepper and roast in the oven for 45 minutes until crispy.

3. For the sauce, blend together the boiled cashews, salsa, garlic, cilantro, nutritional yeast, and salt and black pepper to taste. Add some of the boiled cashew water to help the consistency of the sauce. Add in one sliced shallot after sautéing it in pan for 5 to 7 minutes.

4. Once the purple sweet potatoes are roasted, you can garnish with cilantro and sunflower seeds and serve with the Creamy Spicy Cashew Cream.

Garlic and Herb Avocado Toast

Avocado toast has become one of the most ubiquitous menu items thanks to LA fashion bloggers on Instagram. It is probably one of the most photographed dish at any restaurant. I never order avocado toast because I personally feel the one I make, is the best, and I would never shell out $12 for toast, no matter how fancy it is. This recipe was given to me by my friend, Amisha, and I only modified it slightly, but without her I would be eating regular old sad toast in the morning. Pair this with your favorite brewed coffee and enjoy a relaxing Sunday morning in the comfort of your own home.

- ✎ Prep time 10 minutes
- 🕙 Cook time 7 minutes
- 🍴 Servings 2 servings
- 🕐 Total time 20 minutes

INGREDIENTS

GARLIC AND HERB AVOCADO TOAST

- 5.2 oz Boursin garlic and fine herbs cheese
- Crusty multigrain or sourdough bread
- 1 ripe avocado, sliced
- Cilantro, to garnish
- 1 jalapeño, de-seeded to garnish
- Lemon
- Mike's Hot Honey
- Everything Bagel Spice seasoning

INSTRUCTIONS

1. First slice the multigrain or sourdough bread and toast in the oven until golden and crispy.

2. Spread the Boursin cheese on the toast and then top with the sliced avocados, jalapeños, cilantro, and Everything Bagel Spice seasoning.

3. This step is optional, but it does taste pretty great. Drizzle with Mike's Hot Honey.

4. Enjoy the Garlic and Herb Avocado Toast with your favorite brewed coffee. Seconds are a must.

Cranberry Chutney

This is the best cranberry chutney recipe for Thanksgiving. The orange juice elevates the flavor profile of the chutney, while the black pepper makes for a wonderful bite. Serve this chutney with a mushroom casserole or with your turkey/tofurkey on Thanksgiving.

- Prep time 5 minutes
- Cook time 20 minutes
- Servings 10 servings
- Total time 25 minutes

INGREDIENTS

CRANBERRY CHUTNEY

- 1 12 oz. package of fresh cranberries
- ¾ cup granulated sugar
- ½ cup orange juice
- 1 cup water
- 2 tablespoons black pepper

INSTRUCTIONS

1. In a pan, over medium heat, cook the cranberries in the orange juice, water, sugar and add the black pepper. Bring to a boil and then simmer for 15 to 20 minutes.

2. Garnish with rosemary and serve at your Thanksgiving dinner.

Mansi Akruwala

Cheesy Garlic and Herb Thanksgiving Stuffing

Since Thanksgiving is my favorite holiday, I knew I had to include some of staple recipes for the big day. This stuffing is so cheesy and garlicy, and the fresh herbs really elevate this dish.

- Prep time 5 minutes
- Cook time 20 minutes
- Servings 10 servings
- Total time 25 minutes

INGREDIENTS

CHEESY GARLIC AND HERB THANKSGIVING STUFFING

- 1.5 loaves of Italian bread or any crusty, day old bread will do, cubed
- 2 sprigs rosemary
- 3 sprigs thyme
- 3 tablespoons chopped fresh sage
- 6 cloves, minced or crushed garlic
- 2 tablespoons black pepper
- 3 tablespoons unsalted butter
- 2 shallots, diced
- ¾ cup vegetable broth
- ½ cup of freshly grated parmesan cheese
- ½ cup freshly grated gruyere cheese

INSTRUCTIONS

1. Pre-heat oven to 375 degrees F.

2. In a skillet, melt the butter over medium heat. Stir in the garlic, shallots, and fresh herbs. Add salt to taste. Cook until brown, about 5 minutes.

3. Cube the Italian bread and toss with the sautéed shallots, garlic, and herb mixture. Add in the vegetable broth, which will make the bread very moist. Finally, fold in the parmesan and gruyere cheeses.

4. Bake the stuffing in the oven for 30 minutes until golden, crispy, and the cheese is melted.

5. Serve warm and enjoy at your Thanksgiving dinner

Mansi Akruwala

Creamy Garlic Herbed Mashed Potatoes

Thanksgiving without mashed potatoes just is not a thing, or rather it should be mandated. These creamy garlicy herbed mashed potatoes are a must at any Thanksgiving Dinner. I promise you these mashed potatoes are not dry or lumpy.

- ✎ Prep time 10 minutes
- ⦾ Cook time 20 minutes
- ◷ Servings 12 servings
- ◷ Total time 30 minutes

INGREDIENTS

CREAMY GARLIC HERBED MASHED POTATOES

- 3 ½ pounds Yukon gold potatoes
- 1 cup sour cream, add more to make it creamier
- 4 cloves of roasted garlic, minced or crushed
- 5 oz. Boursin garlic and fine herb cheese
- 5 tablespoons unsalted butter
- Scallions, thinly sliced
- Salt and black pepper to taste

INSTRUCTIONS

1. Peel and dice potatoes and boil until soft, about 20 minutes.

2. Roast the garlic in the oven at 375 degrees F for 20 minutes.

3. Mash the boiled potatoes with the roasted garlic, add in the butter, sour cream, and Boursin cheese. Add salt and black pepper to taste. Fold in thinly sliced green scallions.

4. Serve and enjoy at Thanksgiving.

Creamy Herbed Mushroom Puff Pastry Casserole

This mushroom casserole is the perfect main dish to serve at your vegetarian Thanksgiving. Serve with my Roasted Red Pepper Sauce, and the outcome is too delicious for words to do it justice. Any great dish always has some special sauce that you find yourself scraping the bottom of the bowl for more, or maybe even licking your fingers for that last tasty bite. This sauce is the perfect example of something incredibly versatile and just as delicious paired with a mushroom casserole as it is with some roasted garlic asparagus and creamy mashed potatoes. It really does create the perfect bite. I even serve this with some good toasted crostini, and it is always a hit at any party or family gathering.

- Prep time 10 minutes
- Cook time 35 to 40 minutes
- Servings 8 servings
- Total time 1 hour

INGREDIENTS

CREAMY HERBED MUSHROOM PUFF PASTRY CASSEROLE

- 1 8 oz. package or baby bella mushrooms
- 4 cloves of garlic, minced or crushed
- 2 shallots, diced
- 2 sprigs of fresh rosemary
- 2 sprigs of fresh thyme
- 2 tablespoons fresh sage
- 1 tablespoon vegetable bouillon paste
- 1 teaspoon truffle salt
- 3-4 tablespoons of Boursin garlic and fine herbs cheese
- 2 tablespoons unsalted butter
- ½ CUP OF GRUYERE CHEESE, SHREDDED

ROASTED RED PEPPER SAUCE

- 2 red bell peppers
- 10 almonds
- 1 8 oz. light cream cheese
- 4 cloves of garlic
- Salt and black pepper to taste
- ½ jalapeño, de-seeded

INSTRUCTIONS

1. Pre-heat oven to 400 degrees F and thaw 2 sheets of puff pastry.

2. Roast the red bell peppers for 25 minutes at 425 degrees F. Allow them to cool and then add to a blender with garlic, almonds, and cream cheese. Blend until smooth and creamy. Add salt and black pepper to taste.

3. In a skillet, melt the butter and sauté the garlic until fragrant. Add in the shallots, rosemary, thyme, sage, and vegetable bouillon. Next, add in the sliced mushrooms and cook for 20 minutes until soft and tender. Add in the Boursin cheese and the truffle salt. Allow the filling to cool and set aside.

4. Carefully unroll the puff pastry onto a parchment-lined baking pan. Place the mushroom filling inside. Finally, add in the shredded Gruyere cheese and mix evenly throughout. Top the mushroom filling with the second sheet of puff pastry. Create slits at the top to allow the heat to escape so the casserole does not become soggy and collapse.

5. Bake the casserole in the oven for 35 to 40 minutes, until nice and golden brown and flakey.

Rose Tres Leches Cake

This is one of my favorite desserts that I have made, and it is inspired by the Mexican Tres Leches cake, but with a Middle Eastern or Indian twist. Middle eastern and even Indian desserts are often known to incorporate rose flavoring. Rose offers notes of floral sweetness and is very fragrant. Rose often pairs well with pistachios and the color contrast is often very beautiful and appealing to the eye. For the history buffs, rose petals were introduced by the Persians and have been used in desserts for over 3,000 years. There is some nutritional benefit that comes with roses as well, in the form of antioxidants. I love this recipe not only because of how beautiful it looks and tastes, but it is one of my best kitchen hacks for an easy but impressive dessert. Also, I am no baker so this recipe is for the pros, the novices, and anyone who may be intimidated by the science and precision of baking (hello, me!) The beautiful pink color can be developed naturally with the addition of a beet juice dye or artificially with rose food gel. This dessert offers fragrant rose notes with a hint of sweetness and is so well balanced. It is great for those with a sweet tooth who want to watch their sugar intake.

Pro tip: Serve for dessert after "Cauliflower Shawarma date night".

Mansi Akruwala

- ✎ Prep time 10 minute
- ◔ Cook time 45 minutes
- 🍴 Servings 4
- 🕐 Total time 55 minutes

INGREDIENTS

ROSE TRES LECHES CAKE

- 1 box of moist French vanilla cake mix
- 2 teaspoons vanilla extract
- Edible rose petals, for garnish
- Chopped pistachios, for garnish

ROSE MILKS

- 4 cups whole milk
- 1 12 oz. can of evaporated milk
- 1 pint of heavy cream
- ½ cup sugar
- 2 teaspoons vanilla extract
- 1-2 drops rose food gel or beet juice dye, adjust for desirable color
- ½ cup of rose water

VANILLA-ROSE WHIPPED CREAM

- 1 pint of heavy cream
- 2 teaspoons vanilla extract
- ½ cup powdered sugar, or to taste
- ¼ cup rose water, or to taste

INSTRUCTIONS

1. Pre-heat oven to 375 degrees F.

2. Prepare cake mix first. Follow instructions on the cake mix box-add the eggs and oil accordingly and mix. Then add 2 teaspoons vanilla extract. Bake cake for 45 minutes, follow box instructions for baking times which vary according to pan size and individual ovens.

3. Prepare the tres leches milk mixture. First prepare the homemade condensed milk. I choose to make my own because I can control the sweetness. In a pot, on low heat simmer 2 cups of whole milk, 2 teaspoons

vanilla extract, ½ cup sugar. Let this mixture boil and as it boils it will thicken. You may turn off heat when it begins to boil. Allow this condensed milk to cool on counter or in the fridge before using.

4. In a mixing bowl add in the evaporated milk can, the homemade or store-bought condensed milk, and then the whole milk. Then add 1-2 drops of rose food gel or beet juice dye to achieve desirable pink color.

5. For the rose vanilla whipped cream, take 1 pint of heavy cream and in a stand mixture, whip the heavy whipping cream with vanilla extract, rose water, and powdered white sugar, to taste. The whipped cream will taste very light, airy, and floral with hints of rose and vanilla.

6. After the cake has baked and cooled completely. Make several holes in the cake. Then pour the pink Rose Tres Leches milk mixture on top, creating about 1-2 inches of a pool at the bottom. Then top the cake with the rose-vanilla whipped cream. Finally, decoratively top the cake with the edible rose petals and chopped pistachios.

7. Serve and enjoy this beautifully vibrant pink Rose Tres Leches Cake.

Guava and Cheese Empanadas

I am a big fan of empanadas, which I am sure is apparent considering this is my second empanada recipe in this cookbook. The last family vacation I was able to take was with my parents in 2019 and we traveled all throughout Spain. My favorite cities were Seville, Barcelona, and Granada. We enjoyed the most amazing Sangria in Mallorca and had incredible Spanish riojas in Madrid, especially while watching flamenco dancers at La Taberna de Mister Pinkleton. If you want to see authentic and traditional Spanish flamenco dancers this cute spot is a must and their wines are simply too good. Generous pours are a thing in Europe, especially Spain. These Guava and Cheese Empanadas are the perfect dessert addition to any party and will definitely transport you to Spain.

- Prep time 5 minutes
- Cook time 30 minutes
- Servings 6-8 servings
- Total time 30 minutes

INGREDIENTS

GUAVA AND CHEESE EMPANADAS

- 1 8 oz. package of light cream cheese
- 5 oz. guava paste
- 1 11.6 oz. empanada discs (12 come in a pack)
- Butter

INSTRUCTIONS

1. Pre-heat the oven to 375 degrees F.

2. In the center of the pastry discs put 2 teaspoons of cream cheese and 1 teaspoon of the guava paste and then fold over the empanada. Take a fork and press down on the edges.

3. Brush the empanadas with some butter and bake in the oven for 20 to 25 minutes, until golden brown.

4. Serve and enjoy hot.

Lavender Vanilla and Earl Grey Crème Brulee

I have always been so intimidated by crème Brulee. It seemed like something I could only indulge in, in a fancy French bistro. I promise you, this recipe is completely doable and so delicious. I was inspired by Half Baked Harvest's recipe for Early Grey Crème Brulee, which she described as so easy. In fact, "Easy" was in the recipe title so I knew I could not lose. I love the flavor of lavender, vanilla, and earl grey, so I decided to go with that flavor profile. In fact, on a recent trip to San Francisco, I got to finally try Salt and Straw's Lavendar Honey ice cream and it was incredible. So, this recipe is also inspired by that ice cream.

Thank you, Tieghen for the recipe inspiration.

- ✐ Prep time 30 minutes
- ⏱ Cook time 30 minutes
- 🍴 Servings 4 servings
- 🕐 Total time 5 hours

Mansi Akruwala

INGREDIENTS

Lavender Vanilla and Earl Grey Crème Brulee

- 2 1/2 cups heavy cream
- 1/4 teaspoon salt
- 2 tablespoons loose earl grey tea (teabags can be used too)
- 1 tablespoon culinary grade lavender
- 1 tablespoon vanilla extract
- 5 large egg yolks
- 1/3 cup plus 4 tablespoons granulated sugar

INSTRUCTIONS

1. In a small pot, bring the heavy cream and salt to a low boil until steaming. Remove from the heat. Steep the heavy cream mixture in the earl grey tea (teabags can be used) for 10 minutes.

2. Arrange an oven rack in the middle of the oven. Preheat the oven to 325 degrees F. And then bring 4-6 cups of water to a boil.

3. In a bowl, whisk together the egg yolks and 1/3 cup sugar until combined.

4. Place the steeped heavy cream over medium heat and gently warm until steaming. Remove from the heat and stir in the vanilla. In a slow stream, whisk about 1/2 cup of the cream into the egg yolks, whisking constantly so they do not scramble. Whisk in the remaining cream.

5. Divide the mixture between 4 ramekins. Place the ramekins inside a large lasagna-style baking dish. Fill the dish with boiling water halfway up the sides of the ramekins. Bake for 30 (smaller ramekins) to 40 minutes (larger ramekins), until centers are barely set. Cool completely. Refrigerate 4 hours and up to a couple of days.

6. When ready to eat, top each with 1-2 teaspoons of sugar. Place the ramekins under the broiler and broil until the sugar melts, browns, and then blackens a little, about 5 minutes. You can also use a blow torch.

7. Serve and enjoy, immediately!

Mixed Berry Vanilla and Lemon Chantilly Cream Pie

This is the pie you make for a hot summer day, preferably at a family BBQ. It is the pie that gets devoured and is so delicious. This sugar cookie crust pairs so well with the satin, smooth, and creamy vanilla Chantilly cream which has notes of Vanilla and pops of tart bites from the Meyer lemons. Top it off with some mixed Summer berries and pistachios and you have a party. This would also work well for a bridal shower or an English garden tea party. High tea, British accents, pretentious cucumber sandwiches, and whimsical, elaborate hats not included but always encouraged.

- ✎ Prep time 10 minutes
- ⟳ Cook time 10 to 15 minutes
- 🍴 Servings 8 servings
- 🕐 Total time 1 hour

INGREDIENTS

Sugar Cookie Crust

- 1 cup all purpose flour
- 1 stick (8 tablespoons) unsalted butter, melted
- 1/2 cup sugar
- 2 teaspoons Vanilla extract

Vanilla and Lemon Chantilly Cream

- 1 pint heavy cream
- 3 teaspoons vanilla extract
- 4 oz. light cream cheese
- 4 tablespoons confectioner's sugar, add more for desired sweetness
- 1-2 Meyer Lemons, fresh squeezed juice-adjust according to desired fresh lemony tartness
- Mixed berries (blueberries, raspberries, strawberries, and blackberries) to decorate
- Pistachios, chopped, to garnish

INSTRUCTIONS

1. Pre-heat the oven to 350 degrees F.

2. Melt the butter in a pan. In a medium bowl, combine the flour, butter, sugar, and vanilla extract. In an 8-9-inch glass pie plate, pat down the crust mixture pressing down along the edges of the pie plate. Then bake the crust for 10 minutes. Let cool completely before filling.

3. Meanwhile, make the Vanilla and Lemon Chantilly Cream. In a large bowl, using an electric mixer, beat the heavy cream and vanilla on medium-high speed until soft peaks form, 2 to 3 minutes. Add the cream cheese and powdered sugar and beat until incorporated, 30 seconds. Next, squeeze the juice of a lemon, add more or less depending on desired tartness. I personally go a bit heavy on the lemon, it is so good. I use the juice of two lemons. Chill until ready to use.

4. To assemble, fill the sugar cookie crust with the Vanilla and Lemon Chantilly Cream.

5. Decoratively add the mixed berries on top of the pie. I like to use an assortment of raspberries, blueberries, strawberries, and blackberries. Then top with the chopped pistachios.

6. Serve and enjoy with some tea or coffee at your garden party or BBQ.

Passion Fruit and Rose Chantilly Cream Vanilla Doughnuts

I have to preface this recipe by telling you I am by no means a baker. I do not like baking because of the precision that is involved. With that being said, I am a scientist by heart, but somehow the physician in me will not allow me to measure when I cook. In fact, if I had it my way, I would make a cookbook that simply was a list of ingredients. That would be my dream. Unfortunately, not many people would buy such a cookbook, so alas, I am including precise measurements and attempting more baking. It has to grow on me at some point, right? I cannot stress this enough, but these doughnuts are utterly incredible; I really impressed myself with this recipe. They are light and airy, so flavorful, not too sweet, but oh so decadent and rather fancy. And despite all of this, they are really not that bad to make! Dare I say, they are actually quite easy to make. These are the types of doughnuts you make on an ambitious Sunday morning and serve with the best espresso or cappuccino you can make. Etta James, "A Sunday Kind of Love" is a personal favorite, and a must listen when making these doughnuts. Enjoy these doughnuts, your fresh brewed espresso, and the soulful voice of Etta. Oh, and run, don't walk. You're welcome.

Mansi Akruwala

⟋ Prep time 10 minutes
🕐 Cook time 1 hour
🍴 Servings 20 servings
🕐 Total time 3 hours

INGREDIENTS

PASSION FRUIT ROSE CHANTILLY CREAM

- 1 pint heavy cream
- 1/2-1/4 cup rose water, add more for more rose flavor
- ¼ cup powdered sugar, add more for desired sweetness
- 2 teaspoons vanilla extract
- 3-4 tablespoons of passion fruit puree, found in the frozen section or can be used fresh if in season

STRAWBERRY SUGARED VANILLA DOUGHNUTS

- 3 teaspoons active dry yeast
- 1½ cups 1% warm milk
- ½ cup sugar divided
- 4 tablespoons unsalted butter softened, plus more for greasing
- 1 tablespoon vanilla extract
- 1 tablespoon salt
- 1 whole egg
- 3 egg yolks
- 4¾ cups all purpose flour
- Canola oil for frying
- Strawberry or regular sugar to coat
- Chopped pistachios for garnish
- Lemon zest for garnish

INSTRUCTIONS

1. Sprinkle yeast over the warmed milk and let sit until foamy, about 10 minutes. Once foamy, stir to dissolve.

2. In a stand mixer fitted with a paddle attachment, beat together ½ cup sugar and butter until fluffy, about 3 to 4 minutes.

3. Add yeast mixture, vanilla, salt, egg, and yolks and beat until combined.

4. With the motor running, slowly add flour and beat until all ingredients are incorporated. At this point, the dough will be somewhat sticky. If too sticky to handle, add more flour. The dough should pull away from the sides, while being slightly elastic and sticky.

5. Remove the dough ball and place in a greased bowl and cover loosely with plastic and set in a warm place until doubled in size, about 1 to 2 hours.

6. On a lightly floured surface, gather small pieces of dough and use a 3" cookie cutter or ring and cut into rounds.

7. Transfer rounds to parchment paper-lined baking sheets, about 1" apart.

8. Heat 2 to 3 inches of canola oil in a deep fryer or dutch oven. It should be heated to about 350 degrees F.

9. Working in batches, carefully place the doughnuts in the hot oil and fry, flipping every 30 seconds, until puffed and golden, about 2 to 3 minutes.

10. Toss the fried doughnuts into a bowl with the strawberry or regular sugar and coat them with the sugar. Then sprinkle the chopped pistachios on top.

11. Once the doughnuts have completely cooled, create a hole in the doughnut and then fill with the Passion Fruit and Rose Chantilly Cream with a pastry bag. Alternatively, this cream can be served on the side.

12. Place the doughnuts on a platter, garnish with lemon zest, chopped pistachios, and more strawberry sugar.

13. Enjoy!

Hazelnut Chocolate Espresso Tart

This tart is incredible, thoroughly so impressive, yummy, and just so decadent. The flavors come together so nicely. The crust is so delicious as well. This is the tart you make for Thanksgiving or any given weekend when family or friends are over. It is relatively easy, just has a few extra steps for perfection. Enjoy this Hazelnut Chocolate Espresso Tart with an espresso!

- ✎ Prep time 10 minutes
- ⏱ Cook time 1 hour
- ⏱ Servings 20 servings
- ⏱ Total time 3 hours

INGREDIENTS

TOASTED HAZELNUT CRUST

- 1 cup all purpose flour
- 1 cup roasted hazelnuts, crushed into a powdery mix (Use a food processor blender for this)
- 2 tablespoons light brown sugar
- 2 teaspoons almond extract
- 2 teaspoons vanilla extract
- 2 tablespoons espresso powder
- 1/4 teaspoon baking powder
- 1 teaspoon salt
- 6 tablespoons cold salted butter, cut into chunks

CHOCOLATE HAZELNUT GANACHE FILLING

- ¾ cup heavy cream
- 6 oz. semisweet chocolate chips
- 2/3 cup Nutella or chocolate hazelnut spread
- 1 tablespoon vanilla extract
- 1 teaspoon salt

VANILLA WHIPPED CREAM

- 1 cup heavy cream
- 3 tablespoons confectioner's sugar
- 2 teaspoons vanilla extract
- Toasted hazelnuts, chopped for garnish

INSTRUCTIONS

1. Preheat oven to 350 degrees F.

2. To make the crust, combine the roasted hazelnut powder mixture or meal with the flour, butter, brown sugar, espresso powder, baking powder, salt, and vanilla and almond extracts. The mixture should be crumbly. Take a pie plate and pat down the crust mixture with your hands, to form the crust. Bake for 10-13 minutes. Allow to cook completely before adding the hazelnut chocolate ganache filling.

3. Add the heavy cream and chocolate to a pan and melt until smooth. Refrigerate until ready to use. Must be completely cooled. Once cooled, pour on top of the baked crust. Refrigerate for one hour.

4. For the Vanilla Whipped Cream, use a stand mixer to beat the cream on medium speed until it starts to thicken. Add in the vanilla and confectioner's sugar, and beat until stiff peaks form. Spread the Vanilla Whipped Cream on top of the cool tart. Garnish with chopped hazelnuts.

5. Serve and enjoy with some espresso!

Thank You For Cooking With Me!

Printed in the United States
by Baker & Taylor Publisher Services